Sustaining the Writing Spirit

Holistic Tools for School and Home

2nd edition

Susan A. Schiller

ROWMAN & LITTLEFIELD EDUCATION

A division of
ROWMAN & LITTLEFIELD
Lanham • Boulder • New York • Toronto • Plymouth, UK

Published by Rowman & Littlefield Education
A division of Rowman & Littlefield
4501 Forbes Boulevard, Suite 200, Lanham, Maryland 20706
www.rowman.com

10 Thornbury Road, Plymouth PL6 7PP, United Kingdom

Copyright © 2014 by Susan A. Schiller

All rights reserved. No part of this book may be reproduced in any form or by any electronic or mechanical means, including information storage and retrieval systems, without written permission from the publisher, except by a reviewer who may quote passages in a review.

British Library Cataloguing in Publication Information Available

Library of Congress Cataloging-in-Publication Data

Schiller, Susan A.
  Sustaining the Writing Spirit : Holistic tools for school and home / Susan A. Schiller. — Second edition.
    p. cm.
  Includes bibliographical references and index.
  ISBN 978-1-61048-956-0 (cloth) — ISBN 978-1-61048-957-7 (pbk.) — ISBN 978-1-61048-958-4 (electronic) 1. English language—Composition and exercises—Study and teaching. 2. Creative thinking—Study and teaching. 3. Spirituality—Study and teaching. 4. Holistic education. 5. Education—Philosophy. I. Title.

LB1576.S32535 2014
372.62'3—dc23
                                                                                          2013042435

This book is dedicated to special teachers who taught me to love learning.

Mrs. Fuller, first grade,
Gregory Elementary School

Mrs. Streets, third grade,
Stockbridge Elementary School

Mr. Koljonen, twelfth-grade German teacher,
Thurston High School

Sr. Barbara Johns, Dr. Lynn Schaeffer, Dr. Maureen DesRoches,
and Dr. Frank Rashid,
Marygrove College

Dr. John Brereton, Dr. Barbara Couture, and Dr. Ruth Ray,
Wayne State University

Contents

	Foreword by John P. Miller	vii
	Preface	ix
	Acknowledgments	xiii
Chapter 1	Background and Influential People	1
Chapter 2	Creativity: A Holistic Route to Writing	13
Chapter 3	Spirituality: The Core of Holistic Education	21
Chapter 4	Sustaining Life: Education for Sustainability *Gary Babiuk*	27
Chapter 5	Contemplating Great Things in Soul and Place	45
Chapter 6	Walking in the Spirit of the Medicine Wheel: Learning to See What We Normally Do Not See	53
Chapter 7	Mapping Art and Beauty to Solve Problems	59
Chapter 8	Write Your Own Ending	63
Chapter 9	The Connected Self	67
Chapter 10	Visioning in Silent Community	73
Chapter 11	Screenplay Writing	77

Chapter 12	Info-Commercial	81
Chapter 13	Cave Art: Is It Literature? Is It Writing?	85
Chapter 14	Finding Your Community's Literature	89
Chapter 15	Creating a Life's Legacy	93
Chapter 16	Music and Dance to Inspire the Pen	99
Chapter 17	The Writer's Scrapbook	103
Chapter 18	Voice and Identity: The Sound of Respect	107
Chapter 19	Elements of the Local and Global: Water, Community, and Self *Joy Bracewell*	113
Chapter 20	Writing the Outdoors: Three Days in Nature	117
	Appendix A: Interesting Schools	129
	Appendix B: Rhetorical Aims and Organizational Strategies	135
	Annotated Bibliography	137
	About the Author and Contributors	143

Foreword

In the day of No Child Left Behind, literacy has become a priority in education. Unfortunately, with an emphasis on standardized testing, many approaches to reading and writing are often mechanical as teachers "teach to the test." These approaches may in fact boost test scores in the short term, but we might ask, what do they lead to in the long term? Do current approaches really encourage a love of reading and writing in our students? As Susan Schiller suggests at the beginning of her book, students are often given writing assignments disconnected from their lives, and as a result, there is little engagement in the writing process.

Schiller has developed an approach to writing that engages students holistically as she believes that students "should have the opportunity to use their intellect, their emotion, their spiritual side, their social abilities, and their physical skills; and they should have the opportunity to stretch their awareness of self, of community, and of the world" (preface). For Schiller, writing should be connected to the student's personal talents and interests.

Schiller grounds her work within a holistic perspective that is outlined at the beginning of the book and thus develops a framework for the writing exercises that comprise most of the text. These exercises are designed for the students with whom Schiller works at the postsecondary level, but I believe they could also be adapted to secondary school classrooms. The exercises are teacher friendly as step-by-step guidelines are presented. They also include a variety of techniques such as visualization to stimulate the student's imagination. A number of topics are covered in these chapters and include nature, identity, music and dance, screenplay writing, sustainability, and community.

This book is clearly grounded in Susan Schiller's years of working with these exercises, and teachers using this book can thus feel confident about using them in their own classrooms. Schiller has shown us a way that we can truly engage students in the writing process and also assist their self-awareness and growth as people.

John P. Miller

Preface

Holistic education addresses the whole person within a social and environmental context and perceives all elements of a person—intellectual, physical, emotional, social, and spiritual—as avenues for growth and learning. Holism also moves beyond mainstream conventional approaches that primarily value and rely on logical ways of knowing, ways that condition people to become competitors and consumers. Within educational settings, writing is a natural site for holism because writing is a way of knowing that connects and draws from our inner and outer worlds.

While the purpose of this book is to introduce ideas and activities that encourage holistic education, it also features writing as a way of knowing and as a vehicle by which students may develop relationships between linear and nonlinear ways of seeing the world. This goal has led to an interdisciplinary quality that is invited to arise out of activities contained throughout the book. It has also encouraged spiritual learning that transforms learners when they experience transcendence and awe through creative manifestations.

It is time for writing instructors to bring joy back into the activity and for students to unlearn negative attitudes they might have developed due to conventional approaches. When people write, they should have the opportunity to use their intellect, their emotion, their spiritual side, their social abilities, and their physical skills; and they should have the opportunity to stretch their awareness of self, of community, and of the world. Interconnections should arise naturally. Writers should make choices based on their personal preferences, talents, and interests. Self-satisfaction and effectiveness of the written document should lead any evaluation measures, if they are needed. Grades, or in other words, a reliance on comparisons and competition with others, should be avoided whenever possible.

Exigence and creativity should guide all the rhetorical choices from word choice to voice, goal, and final version. Intuition and emotions should inform the writer and be considered respectful avenues of discovery. The intellect should be blended with emotions and physical ways of finding language. The writer should share with other people and seek social solutions to blocks that might arise along the writing path. Writing needs to be reconceptualized so that it may always be seen as an activity of positive and creative energy. It needs to be activity based and connected to something in the writer's world that allows the writing to be both *desirable* and *worthwhile* to *that* person.

Within most conventional schools and colleges, there is some pressure on teachers to promote what is commonly referred to as "academic writing or academic discourse." This usually means a researched topic, a persuasive aim, a formal voice, and a high degree of critical thinking. Yet, without equal attention given to multiple ways of knowing, including spiritual and emotional intelligence, an imbalance occurs and holistic learning does not emerge.

Moreover, current testing mandates at the state and federal levels encourage the imbalance and by so doing severely thwart self-development and creativity in both teachers and students. In fact, as Peter Elbow likes to remind us, "the structures in mainstream conventional schools often make it harder for good teachers and often do not give them the institutional support they need" (personal communication, February 12, 2007). Teachers and students need a change. It is time for a holistic approach to writing—one that allows the fullest possible range of opportunity for creativity and self-development.

Jane Tompkins, in a *Life in School: What the Teacher Learned*, calls for a "more holistic approach to learning, a disciplinary training for people who teach in college that takes into account the fact that we are educators of whole human beings, a form of higher education that would take responsibility for the emergence of an integrated person" (1996, p. 218). *Sustaining the Writing Spirit* takes a step in that direction by providing a holistic approach that fosters creativity and joy in the doing and producing of written expression. It is not a grammar handbook or a traditional rhetoric or reader but could be used in conjunction with those types of texts. The first four chapters provide background, history, and philosophical reasons for holistic education. While these are helpful to set the context for understanding the motivations driving the rest of the book, writing activities described in subsequent chapters can be experienced prior to reading these early chapters.

Chapter 1 describes holistic education and its historical pioneers. Chapter 2 suggests that teachers and learners should value and use creativity (rather than analysis) as a primary learning strategy. This chapter supports the amount of value placed on creativity in all of the subsequent chapters. Chapter 3 places spirituality at the core of holistic approaches, and chapter 4, offered by Gary Babiuk, a specialist in sustainability, argues that sustainability is essential for changing the world and is a viable holistic pathway for learners. Chapters 5 through 20 present holistic learning activities that provide a context and exigence for writing. Creativity, visual arts, and rhetorical decision making shape the majority of these activities, but all activities attempt to establish a context that provides learners with opportunities to use multiple intelligences and to draw from the spiritual core of the learner. Some of the activities can be completed by individuals writing alone, but many require collaboration among partners or small groups. Step-by-step instructions, prerequisites, safety precautions, materials needed, time desired, and learning goals are also suggested. Most of these activities are flexible, can be easily altered to suit varying ages or skill levels, and can be teacher directed or self-directed. This new edition features two new theoretical chapters (3 and 4), two new activities (chapters 7 and 19), and updates to the holistic school list and annotated bibliography in the appendixes. Joy Bracewell, invited contributor, integrates web-based learning with classroom activity in chapter 19 that complements Gary Babiuk's ideas on sustainability.

At the 2003 Conference on Holistic Education, "Breaking New Ground," keynote speaker Satish Kumar called to holistic educators to focus on a trinity—soil, soul, and society—as a means to organize holistic education. From his viewpoint, these "can inspire a truly holistic thinking. They can bring nature, humanity and spirituality together" (Kumar, 2002, p. 75). Soil comes first because everything we have on earth comes from the soil. It is our role to nourish, care, and preserve the soil in a way that sustains life on our planet. Next, we need to replenish our soul because with a vital soul we can give to the earth and society and know how best to receive gifts from both. Thirdly, we must develop a society based on receiving and giving so that our lives are enriched (Kumar, 2002, pp. 76–78).[1] The activities presented in this book blend aspects of the trinity suggested by Kumar and move away from a focus on organizational strategies as is common in conventional writing instruction.

Appendixes A and B serve as resource material, and an annotated bibliography of suggested reading concludes the book.

Teachers using this book need to be familiar with holistic principles. Background information is especially helpful if a teacher within a mainstream educational environment should need to explain or justify pedagogical decisions. The nonsectarian spiritual center of the holistic approach asks that teachers thus engaged have a personal commitment to their own spirituality and self-development.

Note

1. For a more detailed discussion of Kumar's views on soil, soul, and society, see *You Are Therefore I Am* (2002).

References

Kumar, S. (2002). *You are therefore I am: A declaration of dependence*. Devon, UK: Green Books.

Tompkins, J. (1996). *A life in school: What the teacher learned*. Reading, MA: Perseus.

Acknowledgments

Gary Babiuk's expertise in sustainability is an important new contribution to this edition. Rebecca Zeiss's artistic talent and Clint Burhan's continued acceptance of holistic education have been important to me. I thank them for not giving up on holistic ways of learning. Jennifer Knott's enthusiasm for this project has motivated me more than she knows. Her contribution to the chronology in chapter 1 is invaluable. Conversations and trips shared with Jennifer, Rebecca, and Clint when we attended the Breaking New Ground conferences in Ontario, Canada, have led to insights and epiphanies. Don Backus, Robert Root, Lori Rogers, and Pam Gates are friends and colleagues who have shared expertise and advice throughout the writing of this text. Other inspiring people among my students are Janae Goodchild, Carrie Lake, Carrie Jones, Stephanie Peck, Elizabeth Shamus, Nikki Frazier, Samantha Clark, Tessa Holman, Joel D'Annunzio, Kelly Stevens, and Emily Homrich. Moreover, people who have organized the International Holistic Education Conference: Breaking New Ground serve as beacons to educators who seek fresh new approaches to learning and teaching. Finally, a special thanks goes to my husband, Theopolis L. Gilmore, whose constant faith and love provide a foundation that supports spiritual growth and service to our community.

CHAPTER ONE

~

Background and Influential People

Holistic education is generally perceived as an alternative form of education that concerns the whole learner. Holistic educators believe that the learner's intellect, emotions, physical body, spirit, and social nature develop together rather than independently and that drawing from the whole person is necessary to initiate deep and permanent learning experiences. It is believed that an imbalance occurs in our development if we use one part and not the others. For example, consider people who exercise only the upper body. They might have great strength in the arms but would lack the endurance needed to walk more than a single mile.

Holistic education attempts to integrate all the ways of learning available to us. Inherent social and spiritual characteristics create context within which the mind, emotion, and body are integrated. Within the rich context created by the wholeness, one's spirit assumes a center and vital role because it is the source of our motivation for growth and learning. It is no surprise then that the learner is seen not as an independent agent but rather as a part of the greater whole that includes the family, the community, the natural environment, and the universe (Rocha, 2003, p. xi). Holistic educators use wholeness as a means to teach, and they create methods through which wholeness fosters our full awareness. Our inner and outer lives are no longer isolated but integrated so that we come to a meaningful understanding of our spirit, our soul.

All around the world today, explorative educators are turning to holism as a means to evoke and recover the spiritual center in learners—the center that motivates, awakens, enlivens, and instigates creativity, compassion, honesty, fairness, responsibility, and respect (Lantieri, 2001, p. 6). In the 1980s, Ron Miller's book *What Are Schools For?* presented a historical overview of the socioeconomic political pressures that have shaped most of the current purposes in mainstream public education as well as those educators who sought and created alternative holistic systems for learners.

The time line at the end of this chapter presents a chronological overview of people and ideas in holistic education. John P. Miller's work, *Holistic Teacher* (1993), *The Holistic Curriculum* (1996), and *Education and the Soul* (2000), extended the discussion and featured the spiritual core quite emphatically. In 1997, Regina Paxton Foehr and I edited a collection aimed at teachers of writing in public institutions, *The Spiritual Side of Writing: Releasing the Learner's Whole Potential*, that profiled ways a spiritual approach to teaching can occur without violating the national mandate to separate church and state. Rachael Kessler's *Soul of Education* (2000) has been warmly embraced by educators, and her Passage Ways Institute offers training sessions for educators who wish to move toward a spiritual approach to teaching. Although inspired by wisdom traditions, her work at the institute seeks to remain as neutral as possible so that all worldviews are respected. For example, she offers "solo time" as an alternative practice to meditation in the classroom. During solo time, students are invited to spend time together in silence and stillness with freedom to choose how to be with that silence rather than following specific instructions.

In 2001, Linda Lantieri's edited collection *Schools with Spirit* argued for and provided examples of schools and educators who are successfully placing spirituality at the center of their educational approaches. According to Lantieri, "spiritual experiences can be described as the conscious recognition of a connection that goes beyond our own minds or emotions. It's the kind of experience that sometimes leaves us without words to describe it" (2001, p. 8).

While most people relegate spiritual experiences to sites outside the classroom, holistic educators agree that learners also need opportunities for spiritual experience inside the classroom. Creating learning experiences that evoke the sacred, defined by Parker Palmer as "that which is worthy of respect" (as cited in Lantieri, 2001, p. xiv), is a primary goal among holistic educators. Palmer's seminal book *The Courage to Teach* (1998) is probably by far the most widely read book that advocates a spiritual approach to teaching and learning. Holistic educators believe that the spiritual, the sacred, is not isolated to religious systems but is indeed infused in all daily life, particularly in the soul of the learner. It only needs awakening.

Historical People

The roots of holistic education and philosophy date from Jean Jacques Rousseau, who lived from 1712 to 1778. He observed that "child development proceeds at its own natural pace, which he argued, must be respected because 'the first impulses of nature are always right; there is no original sin in the human heart'" (quoted in R. Miller, 1997, p. 93). Rousseau also believed that the "creative power of the universe . . . God" (R. Miller, 1997, p. 9) is the source of the human personality. Therefore, the human spirit should be respected and included in education. He valued the learner's natural pace of learning and placed it at the heart of holistic education.

Philosophers and education reformers that followed added to Rousseau's principles and argued for changes that would put the learner at the center and within social experiences that used the whole person rather than just the rational intellect.

The Swiss reformer Johann Pestalozzi (1746–1827) created boarding schools that featured farm life. Students lived and worked on farms, and all their learning drew from experiences this environment allowed. Like Rousseau, he also was adamant about teachers respecting students' experiences. Pestalozzi's school became world famous, and educators from various parts of the world came to observe and study his method (R. Miller, 1997, p. 96). A German reformer who worked with Pestalozzi, Friedrich Froebel, went on to create the kindergarten.

In early America, the transcendentalists Ralph Waldo Emerson, Henry David Thoreau, William Ellery Channing, George Ripley, A. Bronson Alcott, and Frances Parker wrote about and advocated school reform that would contain holistic features to the American educational curriculum. The most successful of these men to impact mainstream education was Francis W. Parker, who went to Europe to study the ideas of Pestalozzi and Froebel. Unlike other Americans listed here whose work took place in private schools, Parker's efforts took place in public schools where he served as a superintendent after a long teaching career.

Maria Montessori, an Italian, was educated in medical science and approached learning from within a scientific developmental paradigm. Her work, based on scientific principles, became more influential than her predecessors, and today there are Montessori schools all over the world, with more than three thousand in America alone. Montessori believed that children would naturally select what they wanted to learn and that a teacher's task was to create an inviting environment that provided choice—choices that would promote and develop age-appropriate learning experiences. In a Montessori school, children are encouraged to learn at their own pace and to engage in self-selected learning activities.

In 1919, the owner of the Waldorf cigarette factory in Stuttgart, Germany, asked Rudolf Steiner to create a new school that would contrast mainstream education of the day. Steiner, a well-known writer and philosopher of that time, had already started a movement called anthroposophy, which he defined as "the wisdom of the human being." He believed in reincarnation and thought of education as one means through which we may develop our spirit as it progresses in this life and into the next. Humans, he suggested, are engaged in lifelong learning primarily as an advancement of their spiritual being. Therefore, everything we do in life automatically has a spiritual element in it.[1] Steiner's "Waldorf School" became very successful, and today there are "approximately 750 schools in 44 countries around the world" (Rocha, 2003, p. 77).

The Waldorf approach starts with Steiner's specific ideas regarding spirituality, developmental stages, and the purpose of life on earth. It is not a system that adheres to any particular religious dogma. The curriculum moves in blocks that correspond to the developmental stages of learners, and it is highly stylized to take advantage of the philosophical ideas of Steiner. At least two years of specialized training at a Waldorf teachers' school is required for certification as a Waldorf teacher, and beyond training, teachers are expected to be committed to their own spiritual and professional development. While Waldorf teachers have quite a lot of autonomy, their pedagogical choices must conform to the Waldorf frame and be structured around Steiner's developmental stages and what those imply.

Steiner created an approach that takes advantage of the learning abilities inherent in the three developmental stages he saw; it aims at teaching to the whole child rather than just to the intellect. Steiner believed that developmental stages shift every seven years. During the first stage, the child is thought to be adjusting to the physical body and the physical nature of life. From ages 7 through 14, the child needs to focus on the "feeling life" and on imagination. The third stage, ages 14 to 21, focuses on intellectual development.

Following these stages, children in stage 1 are presented with a curriculum that features a lot of physical learning through the arts, such as drawing, music, dance, and drama. It is believed that children learn best in the morning, so a specific rhythm that draws on this inclination is an important part of the curriculum. Games and physical activity are connected to subject matter whenever possible. Eurythmy, "music and speech expressed in bodily movement," is an important element in a Waldorf school (Rocha, 2003, p. 88). Waldorf teachers receive special training in eurythmy and use it to enhance learning. Children in stage 2 experience opportunities to develop perception, creativity, music, and feelings. It is the stage where feeling and intellect begin to become distinct, but it is not yet a time for intellect to be the focus. Stage 3 provides opportunities to develop intellect and to utilize all that has been carried forward from stages 1 and 2.[2]

The Sudbury Valley School was the first holistic school ever to be fully accredited. It opened in 1968 in Framingham, Massachusetts. Since then, the Sudbury School Network has evolved with schools across the United States.

Sudbury schools are founded on democratic principles and the idea that children learn what they need when they need it. Students and faculty govern the school through decisions made in "meetings" wherein each participant has an equal vote. Classes, like those in mainstream schools, do not exist. Instead, students who are interested in a particular subject approach a faculty member and ask for help in the learning process. The teacher and student(s) enter into a contract once they reach an agreement about curriculum, goals, and time schedules. Children are never "assigned" material they do not ask for. Academic and nonacademic subjects are available. For example, a learner may spend three months in woodworking or cooking, and then switch to math or reading. Daniel Greenberg's book *Free at Last: The Sudbury Valley School* (1987) provides an enjoyable and thorough overview of the school and its principles.

Borrowing from various philosophical tenets found in Waldorf, Sudbury, or Montessori schools, other innovative or alternative schools and learning communities now offer parents and learners choices that go beyond the mainstream approaches found in public schools. The homeschool movement has also gained strength, and today more children are homeschooled in the United States than ever before. *Creating Learning Communities: Models, Resources, and New Ways of Thinking about Teaching and Learning* (R. Miller, 2000) is an excellent source to use as a starting place for learning about these alternative choices.

Philip S. Gang saw connections between Montessori principles and holistic worldviews. He coined the term holistic education and since the mid-1980s has been the leading advocate for the holistic education "movement" around the world. Gang believed that education should

1. give young people a *Vision of the Universe* in which all animate and inanimate beings are interconnected and unified;

2. help students synthesize learning and discover the *interrelatedness of all disciplines*;
3. prepare students for life in the new age by emphasizing a *Global Perspective* and common human interests; and
4. enable the young to develop a sense of harmony and *Spirituality*, which are needed to construct world peace. (Quoted in R. Miller, 1997, pp. 205–206)

In 1991, at the GATE (the Global Alliance for Transforming Education, directed by Gang) conference, a position paper, written by Ron Miller, placed holistic education in a cultural context, expanded Gang's ideas, and introduced ten principles of holistic education that were endorsed by the conference attendees. These educators stated the following:

1. We assert that the primary—indeed the fundamental—purpose of education is to nourish the inherent possibilities of human development.
2. We call for each learner—young and old—to be recognized as unique and valuable. . . . Each individual is inherently creative, has unique physical, emotional, intellectual, and spiritual needs and abilities, and possesses an unlimited capacity to learn.
3. We affirm what the most perceptive educators have argued for centuries: education is a matter of experience. Learning is an active multisensory engagement between an individual and the world. . . .
4. We call for wholeness in the educational process, and for the transformation of educational institutions and policies required to attain this aim. Wholeness implies that each academic discipline provides merely a different perspective on the rich, complex, integrated phenomenon of life.
5. We hold . . . that educators ought to be facilitators of learning, which is an organic, natural process and not a product that can be turned out on demand.
6. We call for meaningful opportunities for real choice at every stage of the learning process.
7. We call for a truly democratic model of education to empower all citizens to participate in meaningful ways in the life of the community and the planet.
8. We believe that each of us—whether we realize it or not—is a global citizen. . . . We believe that it is time for education to nurture an appreciation for the magnificent diversity of human experience. . . .

9. We believe that education must spring organically from a profound reverence for life in all its forms. We must rekindle a relationship between the human and natural world that is nurturing, not exploitive.
10. The most important, most valuable part of the person is his or her inner, subjective life—the self or the soul.... We believe that education must nourish the healthy growth of the spiritual life, not do violence to it through constant evaluation and competition. (Quoted in R. Miller, 1997, p. 205)

Adding to the direction provided by GATE, the Holistic and Aesthetic Education Graduate Focus at the Ontario Institute for Studies in Education at the University of Toronto (OISE UT) has held international conferences on holistic education. *Holistic Learning and Spirituality in Education*, a collection edited by John P. Miller and colleagues (2005), features the work of selected conference presenters from the first three. This collection, perhaps more than any other, establishes holistic education as a wise and spiritual approach to learning.

A Brief Chronology

1762 Jean Jacques Rousseau argued that education should seek a connection between the "organic needs of human development and the rational requirements of the 'social contract'" (quoted in R. Miller, 1997, p. 92).

1809 Johann Pestalozzi further developed Rousseau's theory. He used working farms as schools for students, mainly orphans, and taught them that "God's nature which is in you is held sacred in this House. We do not hem it in; we try to develop it. Nor do we impose on you our own natures.... Under our guidance you should become men such as your natures—the divine and sacred in your nature—require you to be" (quoted in R. Miller, 1997, p. 98).

1826 Friedrich Froebel writes *The Education of Man*, after working for a few years with Pestalozzi. In this book he comes up with three central holistic themes: (1) Every person has the ability to unfold divinely. (2) The divine unfolding comes from a spontaneous creative nature in people. (3) The educational environment should respect the fullness and natural stages of his unfolding (quoted in R. Miller, 1997, pp. 99–100). Froebel is best remembered for creating the kindergarten.

1830   The New England transcendentalism movement began. This movement addressed issues of religion, philosophy, politics, education, and social improvements. Many of the most influential thinkers in transcendentalism promoted a holistic approach to living.

1834   A. Bronson Alcott started a school in the Masonic Temple: the Temple School. He worked with William E. Channing and was a radical transcendentalist. He hated materialism and believed that education must "nurture the full development of the human powers of each child" (quoted in R. Miller, 1997, p. 114).

1837   Henry David Thoreau studied with Ralph Waldo Emerson. He taught for a brief time but left to live at Walden pond. While he wrote on many philosophical topics, within education, he thought that the teacher should find as much to learn from the student as the student has to learn from the teacher. This idea is a central concern in holistic education.

1839   William E. Channing, or "The Great Awakener," a preacher for the Unitarian movement, wrote that education starts with the child's nature and not the educators' preconceptions. Like Froebel, Pestalozzi, and Rousseau, he believed in the divine awakening within people, especially children.

1840   Beginning of the American industrial revolution, which spurred the Civil War and end of slavery. This change also brought on many new radical thinkers and ideas.

1850   Ralph Waldo Emerson, a major figure in transcendentalism, said, "the secret of education lies in respecting the pupil. It is not for you to choose what he shall know, what he shall do. It is chosen and foreordained, and he only holds the key to his own secret" (quoted in R. Miller, 1997, p. 108).

1861   Rudolf Steiner is born. He was an Austrian educator who wrote many books on philosophy, economics, education, and social conditions. He later founded the Waldorf Schools.

1870   Maria Montessori is born. She was a premier leader of holistic alternative education. Montessori was the first Italian woman to enter into medical school. She began working with disabled children, whether they were mentally retarded or had learning disabilities, and with these children she discovered new ways to teach and enhance their learning abilities.

1894   Francis W. Parker, a public school educator, brought significant attention to holistic methods with his book *Talks on Pedagogies*, which focused on the dignity of human nature.

1901	Francisco Ferrer, a radical anarchist, started a school in Barcelona, the "Modern School." He was deeply influenced by Rousseau, Tolstoy, and the British anarchist William Godwin.
1907	Maria Montessori begins her educational theory work with the children in slum areas. She believed that the spiritual development of children was as important as the learning of books.
1910	The Francisco Ferrer Association is founded.
1913	Steiner starts his own movement, anthroposophy. A core idea in anthroposophy is that "the inner life of humans, the soul, contains the deepest truths of human existence" (quoted in R. Miller, 1997, p. 169).
1919	Steiner founded the Waldorf Schools.
1921	A. S. Neill founded Summerhill School in England.
1947	UNESCO is an agency of the United Nations that promotes collaboration among nations through a focus on education, science, and culture. It traces its roots to the League of Nations formed in 1921 and the first International Bureau of Education formed in 1925. A stronger focus that has been consistent to date began in 1947. Their broadest goal is to make basic education available to all people in all nations by 2015. Numerous affiliate organizations focus on specific areas of interest.
1968	The first Sudbury School is opened.
1969	The Albany Free School opens in Albany, New York.
1970	The open classroom movement becomes controversial. The open classroom provides teachers, parents, and students with an equal voice in participation and administration of school affairs.
1971	Jean Piaget's theory of child development becomes widely discussed.
1972	The free school movement is developed. More people are looking at alternative ways to educate and are withdrawing their children from schools and forming "free schools" or "open schools."
mid-1980s	Steiner's Anthroposophy Society is extended to Japan. Fifty-eight books by Japanese authors are published on Waldorf education.
1980s	The term "holistic education" is presented systematically, but independently, by American educator Ron Miller and by Canadian educator John P. Miller.
1988	The inaugural edition of *Holistic Educational Review* (HER) is issued. Edward T. Clark Jr. writes a seminal article in the *Holistic Educational Review* titled "The Search for a New Educational Paradigm." This article approaches new ways of managing and structuring schools, teaching, and learning.

1989   The Alternative Education Resource Organization is founded by Jerry Mintz to promote student-driven, learner-centered approaches to education. Their first annual conference is held in 2004.
1990   The Chicago Statement on Education comes out of a retreat of eighty holistic educators.
        GATE, the Global Alliance for Transforming Education, is directed by Philip Gang. Several conferences were held in the next few years.
1991   GATE releases a position paper titled "Education 2000: A Holistic Perspective."
1993   The first International Democratic Education Conference (IDEC) was held in Israel. This annual conference is manifested by members of the International Democratic Education Network (IDEN) and is dedicated to promoting the Democratic Education Movement around the world. Each conference is "hosted" by a different country, organized by various schools or other organizations such as AERO (Alternative Educational Resource Organization); in some cases, the conference has been completely organized by students. The 2013 conference was held in Boulder, Colorado.
1996   John P. Miller's book *The Holistic Curriculum*, is published.
1997   Twenty educators meet at the University of Nottingham in the UK for two days of seminars on the future of education and its evolution. The conference is known as the Nottingham Conference for Education in 2020.
        The first conference at the Ontario Institute for Studies in Education at the University of Toronto (OISE UT) is held on holistic education: International Holistic Education Conference: Breaking New Ground, Toronto. This conference is held every two years.
2000   Over a million families in the United States now homeschool their children.
2002   The ministry of education in Japan included new aspects into their education. The three key words in this new aspect are "*kokoro-no-kyoiku* (education for the heart and soul), *sogo-gakushyu* (integrated learning), and *tokushyoku, koseika* (the uniqueness of each school as well as of the individual person)" (J. P. Miller et al., 2005, pp. 130–131).
2005   *Holistic Learning and Spirituality in Education*, edited by John P. Miller, Selia Karsten, Diana Denton, Deborah Orr, and Isabella Colalillo Kate, is published. It features presentations from three International Holistic Education Conference: Breaking New Ground meetings.

2007   The Association for Supervision and Curriculum Development (ASCD) launches a worldwide initiative titled "Whole Child," which aims to change educational practices and policies to ones that encompass aspects of the whole learner. Educators are asked to focus on education that ensures the student is healthy; safe, engaged, supported, and challenged. To integrate these goals, ASCD creates professional development opportunities for educators to discuss ways to do this within the school climate and culture; the curriculum and instruction; leadership, family and community engagement, and assessment; and professional development and staff capacity. While holistic approaches are embedded, they are not the main point of discussion, and at times ASCD approaches appear more traditional than holistic. Yet, the focus on the whole child supports holistic education, especially when exploring ways students may be emotionally supported, engaged, and encouraged to develop as healthy individuals.

2012   Bhutan is at this time the only country in the world that has explicitly adopted holistic education as part of its educational policy. On April 2, John P. Miller was invited to a one-day meeting at the United Nations in New York. The main objective of this meeting was to support a statement that was developed by the government of Bhutan on a new economic paradigm based on happiness and well-being. The statement is entitled "Realizing a World of Sustainable Well-Being and Happiness." It includes the statement that education should promote "holistic life-long learning, including vital literacies required for wellbeing, such as ecological, civic, cultural, health, nutrition, science, financial, and other literacies."

2013   UNESCO Asia Pacific Network for International Education and Values Education (APNIEVE) held a conference on holistic education in 2013.

Notes

1. For a fuller discussion of Steiner's views, see Rocha (2003), *Schools Where Children Matter: Exploring Educational Alternatives*.

2. See *Waldorf Education: Reflections on the Essentials* by Jeffrey Kane (2002) for a detailed description of all three stages.

References

Alternative Educational Resource Organization (AERO). (2013, June 28). Join the education revolution. Retrieved from www.educationrevolution.org/.

Asia Pacific Network for International Education and Values Education (APNIEVE). (2013, June 29). Home page. Retrieved from www.unesco-apnieve.edu.au/.

Association for Supervision and Curriculum Development (ASCD). (2003, July 1). The Whole Child Initiative. Retrieved from www.ascd.org/whole-child.aspx.

Foehr, R. F., & Schiller, S. A. (Eds.). (1997). *The spiritual side of writing: Releasing the learner's whole potential*. Portsmouth, NH: Heinemann Boynton Cook.

Greenberg, D. (1987). *Free at last: The Sudbury Valley School*. Framingham, MA: Sudbury Valley School Press.

International Democratic Education Conference (IDEC). (2013, June 29). IDEC 2013: What future do you want to create? Retrieved from www.idec2013.org/.

Kane, J. (2002). Waldorf education: Reflections on the essentials. In J. P. Miller & Y. Nakagawa (Eds.), *Nurturing our wholeness: Perspectives on spirituality in education* (pp. 241–263). Brandon, VT: Foundation for Educational Renewal.

Kessler, R. (2000). *The soul of education*. Alexandria, VA: Association for Supervision and Curriculum Development.

Lantieri, L. (Ed.). (2001). *Schools with spirit: Nurturing the inner lives of children and teachers*. Boston: Beacon.

Miller, J. P. (1993). *Holistic teacher*. Toronto: Ontario Institute for Studies in Education Press.

Miller, J. P. (1996). *The holistic curriculum*. Toronto: Ontario Institute for Studies in Education Press.

Miller, J. P. (2000). *Education and the soul*. Albany, NY: State University of New York Press.

Miller, J. P., et al. (Eds.). (2005). *Holistic learning and spirituality in education*. Albany, NY: State University of New York Press.

Miller, R. (1991). *New directions in education: Selections from Holistic Review*. Brandon, VT: Holistic Education Press.

Miller, R. (1997). *What are schools for? Holistic education in American culture* (3rd rev. ed.). Brandon, VT: Holistic Education Press.

Miller, R. (Ed.). (2000). *Creating learning communities: Models, resources, and new ways of thinking about teaching and learning*. Brandon, VT: Foundation for Educational Renewal.

Palmer, P. J. (1998). *The courage to teach: Exploring the inner landscape of a teacher's life*. San Francisco: Jossey-Bass.

Rocha, D. L. D. (2003). *Schools where children matter: Exploring educational alternatives*. Brandon, VT: Foundation for Educational Renewal.

United Nations Educational, Scientific, and Cultural Organization (UNESCO). (2013, July 28). Home page. Retrieved from www.unesco.org/

CHAPTER TWO

~

Creativity

A Holistic Route to Writing

Mainstream writing programs in institutions of higher education across the United States are generated by a long tradition of separating creativity from logical ways of knowing. In composition courses, academic discourse dominates the curriculum, even though it is only one rhetorical form.[1] Indeed, most writing programs are built around the goal of competency in it.

In large state colleges and universities, English departments routinely offer fifty to one hundred or more sections of freshman composition compared to one freshman-level creative writing course. Students are required to take one, two, sometimes three courses of composition, while creative writing courses generally only fulfill electives. Unfortunately, the majority of students *never* study creative writing. In fact, creativity is rarely taught or promoted and might even be penalized in composition programs. An intense and provocative dichotomy between creativity and logical ways of knowing is sustained, and it permeates education to such a degree that, when questioned, is done so in an environment of suspicion and stigma.

Within this system, almost all students learn to place a higher value on research than on creativity or on professions within the arts such as dance, music, or drama. Western cultures tend to perceive careers in artistic fields as those that are less financially stable than, for example, a career in law, medicine, or business, choices that typically rely on linguistics and logic as the primary way of knowing. Students learn to rely on analysis and argumentation. Analysis and argumentation are rhetorical acts wherein the parts are separated from the whole for closer scrutiny of their solitary function within the whole, not for their interconnections with other parts. In analysis, the sum of the parts equals the total of the whole.

Moreover, this view (and practice of) analysis contains a reductionist quality that weakens the act of knowing. This quality is too restrictive and causes writing to become an arduous time-intensive task that allows little room for original thought or creativity, especially when it becomes the primary element or preferred model for knowing. It is not holistic because it relies on logical and linguistic ways of knowing, and features disconnections rather than interconnections.

Analysis or argumentation from a holistic perspective sees the sum of the parts as greater than the total of the whole. In fact, the whole cannot be completely understood solely by investigating the parts; we must also review and understand the connections within the parts, the connections within the whole, and the connections to the exterior elements surrounding the whole. The connections and inclusion of the exterior elements enrich the phenomenon and enliven knowledge making.

Within mainstream education, but differing from composition programs, creative writing programs move beyond the logical and linguistic ways of knowing to include and connect with creative processes of the writers. As students discover their own creative processes, they learn that the act of creativity *refreshes their soul and then ignites cognition*; objective data simply functions to support and supplement the creative impulse. They learn to value creativity as highly as, or even more highly than, logical and linguistic ways of knowing. As a result, students inculcate a reliance and dependence *on their ability to be creative* and the creative process becomes *a routine natural way of learning*. This is a holistic way of learning that balances multiple intelligences; it includes a broader field of rhetorical and social choices, and it connects writers to them.

Unfortunately, within mainstream education today, information, logic, and persuasion, the essential modes in research, still receive more value than does creativity, despite the work in multiple ways of knowing documented by Howard Gardner. Although Gardner's seven types of intelligence, "linguistic, logical mathematical, spatial, musical, kinesthetic, interpersonal, and intrapersonal" has received general acceptance,[2] mainstream education still relies primarily on linguistic and logical mathematical ways of knowing (quoted in J. P. Miller, 1993, p. 20; Noddings, 1992, p. 31). This seems to be most unwise considering what we know about creativity. We need to move closer to a holistic form of education—one that values creativity, rather than analysis, as the primary learning strategy—and one that is made available to large numbers of students, particularly students of writing.

Modifications to existing writing programs that would transform the logic and linguistic basis to one that is more holistic is not necessarily a difficult thing to do if we focus on the use of creativity as the primary learning strategy. We do not need to cut or replace composition courses with creative writing courses; we need to *redesign* composition courses so that creativity can *dominate* the curriculum in a way that also invites objective data to function in a *supportive* role. First, a working definition of creativity should inform and frame the new design, and secondly, the creative process(es) should be identified so that writers have a clear behavioral model to inform their decisions.

Activity in the field of creativity studies (what it is and how it works) has increased over the last seventy years and is usually dominated by psychology. Social, psychological, emotional, cultural, and biological factors are most often featured. Studies tend to fall into two categories: idiographic research that relies on individual case studies and nomothetic research that seeks discovery of general or universal laws that can be applied to all (Gardner, 1994, p. 143).[3]

Gardner's writing, attempting to construct a bridge that spans idiographic and nomothetic research, presents a more holistic perspective, although he fails to account for the spiritual side of knowing. He stresses cognitive and developmental psychological frames that take into account social and motivational aspects of creativity. His approach is "inherently interdisciplinary"—a feature that leans toward holism (1994, p. 145). About his definition and approach, Gardner says,

1. I focus equally on problem solving, problem finding, and the creation of products, such as scientific theories, works of art, or the building of institutions.
2. I emphasize that all creative work occurs in one or more domains.[4] Individuals are not creative (or noncreative) in general; they are creative in particular domains of accomplishment and require the achievement of expertise in these domains before they can execute significant creative work.
3. No person, act, or product is creative or noncreative in itself. Judgments of creativity are inherently communal, relying heavily on individuals expert within a domain. (1994, p. 145)

Gardner's view requires a broadening of perspective that lets us see that "creativity emerges in virtue of a dialectical process among *individuals* of talent, *domains* of knowledge and practices, and *fields* of knowledgeable judges" (1994, p. 146). His work further relies on two general positions: (1) people can develop all seven intelligences he has already identified, and (2) creative people "are characterized particularly by a tension, or lack of fit, between the elements involved in a productive work" (p. 146). He labels this tension *fruitful asynchrony* and says it is "the conquering of these asynchronies that leads to the establishment of work that comes to be cherished" (p. 146).[5] In other words, fruitful asynchrony provides the initiating impulse for creativity. What does this mean for people who seek to produce a piece of writing? Let's move through Gardner's three phases of creativity to see.

First, writing can be identified as problem solving or the creation of a product (the written document). The beginning step is to decide which one or if both task descriptors apply.

Second, the domain, or set of practices one needs, should be identified. Then writers can determine whether or not their expertise is sufficient or if it needs development before the creative work is manifested. In many instances, actions taken to manifest the creative work increase the level of expertise and these actions may be self-motivated by the creator or externally motivated by an expert in the domain.

Third, since judgments of creativity are inherently communal, writers need connections with experts within the domain that can articulate previously set standards for determining the emergence of creativity. Standards might also serve to direct the creative action. For some people, standards might actually inhibit creativity if they cannot imagine meeting or surpassing them. For other people, the standards may appear too limited and too easy to meet or surpass. In this case, the standards might initiate a new level of achievement, but if the achievement is too extreme to the community of judges, a different type of tension can arise. The cliché often applied to such people is that they are "ahead of their time." Yet, many of our greatest thinkers and creators have been labeled as such and have depended on their own standards; they become their own judges and work to please their own innate need to create something new.

It is easy to see that fruitful asynchrony can begin in all three categories and that no person, act, or product is creative or noncreative in itself. Since elements in the creative act are interconnected, holism is strong. Moreover, the creative act in all of the three categories requires writers to *imagine* they can accomplish something new.

At the root of "imagine" is "image." According to the research completed on imagery and creativity by George Ainsworth-Land, the relationship between creativity and imagery is developmental. People can identify and use a creative process:

1. The first impulse is sense related and arises out of physical need.
2. The second involves improvement of an idea or artistic product through analysis and evaluation.
3. The third requires synthesis not just revision or modification. Something new or novel must be discovered through the synthesis before there is a breakthrough to new knowledge or understanding.
4. The final step, Ainsworth-Land states, occurs when "one's whole being comes into play with the conscious and unconscious minds, reason and intuition, inner and outer, subsumed into a kind of meta-consciousness. . . . The self is part of a larger reality. [Here, one is] building new perceptual order" (quoted in J. P. Miller, 1996, p. 94). This holistic process casts creativity as a self-motivated action that connects the individual inner life of the creator with the exterior social and environmental exigencies described so thoroughly by Gardner. Both Gardner and Ainsworth-Land provide models that can help us understand and implement creativity as the primary and dominant strategy for writing, regardless of any specific rhetorical genre we seek to produce.

The process described by Ainsworth-Land *naturally* activates learning, and with creativity as the dominant strategy, students awaken to the innate and universal human desire for learning. When students complete a creative project, they naturally combine analytic thinking, critical thinking, research, creativity, and reflection. They must imagine their project completed and then attempt to reach the image they have mentally created. As they reach toward completion, they participate physically and socially when choosing collaboration with peers and then again during the presentations of their completed projects.

Their intellect and spirit are awakened by work they choose, create, and design, and their intellectual abilities are stretched with the challenge of synthesizing material into a creative artifact that they judge to be aesthetically pleasing. A transcendent unity occurs when, through the creative impulse, these parts of the learner are integrated and harmonized within their expressive project.

Through creativity, students further develop a holistic worldview—one that provides "an ability to see connections between diverse things and see the bigger picture" (Zohar & Marshall, quoted in Lantieri, 2001, p. 17). Students also have an opportunity to develop spiritual intelligence,[6] which Danah Zohar and Ian Marshall define as "intelligence with which we address and solve problems of meaning and value, the intelligence with which we can place our actions and our lives in a wider, richer meaning-giving context. It is the intelligence with which we can assess that one course of action or one life path is more meaningful than another" (quoted in Lantieri, 2001, p. 18). Zohar and Marshall "call spiritual intelligence the ultimate intelligence because it is the necessary foundation for the effective functioning of the other intelligences and because it has a transformative power" (p. 18).

The separation of church and state is a highly regarded mandate that most mainstream public schools maintain. Holistic educators seek the same goal and offer multiple definitions for secular spiritual approaches to education. For example, Linda Lantieri says, "Spiritual experience can be described as the conscious recognition of a connection that goes beyond our own minds or emotions," and spiritual approaches are "the kinds of approaches that encourage a commitment to matters of the heart and spirit that are among the positive building blocks of healthy development" (2001, p. 16). Parker Palmer tells us the spiritual voice is "the voice of soul, that sacred place in every human being where suffering is transformed into creativity and from which generosity can flow" (quoted in Lantieri, 2001, p. 132). John P. Miller writes in *The Holistic Curriculum* that spirituality is the "sense of awe and reverence for life that arises from our relatedness to something both wonderful and mysterious" (1996, p. 2). This is similar to Ron Miller's statement that spirituality is "some even larger dimension of cosmic purpose, which many people term as the 'spiritual' dimension" (2000, p. 11).

My own definition is not so different from these. I believe a spiritual pedagogy is founded upon and develops our wonder and awe of the infinite mystery of the cosmos, of all people and gifts of the earth, and of our mental, physical, emotional, and creative abilities. From just these few working definitions, we can see that spirituality is easily identifiable outside of religion; it is a flexible and varied topic that can sustain and enrich education.

Creativity as a dominant learning strategy fosters an environment where the "basic [human] need to create" can thrive (Gifford, 1956, p. 32). Creativity also facilitates a spiritual approach to learning because it requires learners to connect their inner being, their soul, to their exterior world. It asks that they find meaning and purpose in what they do—it evokes holism.

Notes

1. Academic discourse usually refers to writing that takes the forms of argumentation, objective data reporting, and research-based prose. A formal third-person voice is almost always used. Subjective and/or emotional content such as anecdotes or personal opinions are not permitted.

2. Gardner's work helped open doors for others to later research and identify emotional intelligence and spiritual intelligence.

3. For a fuller view of creativity studies, see Boden (1994).

4. "A domain is a set of practices associated with an area of knowledge; the field consists of the individuals and institutions that render judgments about work in a domain" (Gardner, 1994, p. 152).

5. In this study, Gardner goes on to use even well-known creators: Sigmund Freud, Albert Einstein, Pablo Picasso, Igor Stravinsky, T. S. Eliot, Martha Graham, and Mahatma Gandhi—each exemplifying at least one of the seven intelligences Gardner identifies.

6. Gardner's intelligences, developed within cognitive psychology, do not include spiritual intelligence. Within the field of holistic education, however, spiritual intelligence is essential. Without the spiritual core, there is no holism.

References

Amabile, T. M. (1983). *The social psychology of creativity.* New York: Springer-Verlag.

Boden, M. A. (Ed.). (1994). *Dimensions of creativity.* Cambridge, MA: MIT Press.

Gardner, H. (1994). The creators' patterns. In M. A. Boden (Ed.), *Dimensions of creativity* (pp. 143–158). Cambridge, MA: MIT Press.

Gifford, D. (1956). The creative process in the classroom. Paper presented at Conference on Creativity as a Process. Arden House, Harriman, NY, October 10–12.

Lantieri, L. (Ed.). (2001). *Schools with spirit: Nurturing the inner lives of children and teachers.* Boston: Beacon.

Michalko, M. (2001). *Cracking creativity: The secrets of creative genius.* Berkeley, CA: Ten Speed Press.

Miller, J. P. (1993). *Holistic teacher.* Toronto: Ontario Institute for Studies in Education Press.

Miller, J. P. (1996). *The holistic curriculum.* Toronto: Ontario Institute for Studies in Education Press.

Miller, R. (Ed.). (2000). *Creating learning communities: Models, resources, and new ways of thinking about teaching and learning.* Brandon, VT: Foundation for Educational Renewal.

Noddings, N. (1992). *The challenge to care in schools: An alternative approach to education.* New York: Teachers College Press.

CHAPTER THREE

Spirituality

The Core of Holistic Education

If we call ourselves holistic teachers, it means we engage spirit, and spirit is at the core of our theories and practices. It means we try to engage the whole learner by touching multiple ways of knowing and learning, including the visual, verbal, physical, intellectual, emotional, social, environmental, and spiritual. The trickiest one here is that which we name *spiritual*.

The word *spiritual* is a loaded word in nearly the same way as the word *God*. When *spiritual* is used, most listeners link to *God* and expect some connection to fundamentalism, proselytizing, or a specific dogma. People automatically think and feel religion and such thoughts are either positive or negative depending on their personal foreground. It is just the way it is, a point of rhetorical reality. But as a scholar and educator trying to approach spirituality in education, I know that one's way of receiving the word *spiritual* is constructed and shaped by cultural conditioning.

Over the years, I have learned that using the word *spiritual* as a *secular* construct always requires a parenthetical definition with new attributes such as awe, inspiration, creativity, transcendence, and joy in learning. Once people accept new ways of speaking about what it means to be "spiritual," traditional education can change and become holistic. This sounds easier than it is, for cultural conditioning places people in deep grooves from which they perceive the world, and these grooves are strongly in place by adolescence.

Moreover, as teachers, we must see the groove and be able to step out of it before we can ask others to do the same. This means that it is essential for holistic teachers to practice what they preach—that they base their teaching practices on their own consciousness and spirit-based lifestyle.

If we call ourselves holistic teachers, it means we have made a serious and lifelong commitment not just to our own self-development but also to philosophies that inform our practices, to the students entrusted to us, to the communities in which we work and live, and to the goal of changing our world for the better. It means we value creativity, sustainability, multiple ways of knowing, awakening the inner being in each of us, and living a life based on compassion, tenderness, love, and wisdom. Respect for all the faces of humankind is paramount as is the idea that people are transformed from the inside out.

Holistic educators seek to touch the soul, to awaken the excitement of growth and the empowerment that comes with knowledge. We seek the connections among all life so that we might better sustain life. We believe in transcendence; by this, I mean powerful moments that show us deeper dimensions in life. From this philosophical position, we attempt to create conditions for students wherein transcendence is invited and may occur.

A spiritual pedagogy is founded upon and develops our wonder and awe of the infinite energy of the cosmos—an energy tapped by us when we blend our inner and outer ways of knowing in creative acts that result in wonder-filled manifestations. When such manifestations inspire awe in ourselves and in others, we have engaged the spiritual side of learning.

While most people relegate spiritual experiences to sites outside the classroom, holistic educators agree that learners also need opportunities for spiritual experience inside the classroom. Holistic educators believe that the spiritual, the sacred, is not isolated to religion but is indeed infused in all daily life, particularly in the soul of the learner. It only needs awakening. So, how can we do that?

It is possible to awaken the spirit through creativity, transcendence of limitations, and meditation. Transcendence happens when the spirit awakens to and accepts change. Transcendence requires removing resistance or fear to new ideas. It requires a curious mind that is unafraid to encounter the unknown until it is known. It requires trust that something beautiful lays ahead. As presented in chapter 2, creativity is a learned process that contains the power to evoke awe and wonderment. Meditation, also a learned process, can take multiple forms, but each invites reflective contemplative conditions from which creativity may be ignited and transcendence may flow.

Transcendence is rarely discussed in traditional approaches because, even though it may be placed in contexts other than religion, it also holds some of the same connotative associations as the word *spiritual*. *Meditation* can also be a word that raises religious connotations, although as the twenty-first century moves ahead, it seems the word is less loaded than it was forty or even twenty years ago.

However, even among holistic educators, a meditation practice can be labeled differently in an effort to bypass religious connotations. For example, it might be called "silent time," "mindfulness practice," "reflection practice," or simply "contemplation." Choosing the term for meditation is a matter of personal comfort. The type of school and course in which meditation is integrated establishes boundaries for the educational context and purpose and can also assert influence over the term chosen. Additionally, the types of students must be considered. Students who have been homeschooled or have experienced Waldorf, Montessori, Sudbury, or free schools are likely to be comfortable with the word *meditation*.

On the other hand, students in state universities or community colleges with no experience with contemplative ways of thinking are often shy of meditation or in some cases even afraid of it. Yet when asked to practice "silent time" or "reflection practice" with a stated purpose for its inclusion in the course, they may engage it more willingly and with less trepidation.

A distinction between visualization practices and meditation is helpful at this point, since most students, especially those who are athletes, have been introduced to "visualization activities." In visualizations, students are "guided" through an inner-imaging process that is prompted by a script or set of suggestions delivered by the teacher or coach. Students who have experienced visualizations in a positive way typically have learned to see themselves as winners or as meeting specific goals.

However, there are students who have had negative experiences with visualizations and do not want to experience them again. It is important to note that meditation, an inner silent practice to quiet the mind and body as well as to increase self-awareness, is not a "guided" activity or a "visualization" aimed at specific outcomes. James Moffett, author of *The Universal Schoolhouse*, once told me that he never used visualizations because he did not want to "plant" ideas or images into people. Yet, John P. Miller uses visualizations with his students and recommends them in his book *The Holistic Teacher*. I have used both and prefer to keep them separated as two different avenues to spiritual learning. I have found visualizations helpful within an appropriate context and purpose, but I don't use them to replace meditation. Meditation is the foundational practice that leads to transcendence, self-awareness, and creativity. And, yes, transcendence, self-awareness, and creativity can and do occur in the absence of a meditation practice, but when supported and/or initiated by meditation, they are quicker, easier, and less strained.

Developing a personal meditation practice is another matter of personal choice. There are various forms to choose, and whether people practice one or many is entirely up to them. People might decide to experience several before choosing a single practice or might wish to integrate more than one into their daily life. The main thing to remember about meditation is that the practice itself is not the reason to practice; the reason to practice is to develop a more peaceful and integrated lifestyle so that wonder and awe can be experienced in even the smallest daily event. With practice, one learns how to live a contemplative life in all that is demanded each day. It is vital for teachers to understand the challenges and joys of living a contemplative life if they are to encourage students to experience a spiritual approach to learning. We expect math, science, and English teachers to be prepared with a knowledge of their discipline; likewise, we need to expect the same from teachers who use a spiritual approach.

Presenting students with an overview of meditation types is a useful starting point. Two texts by John P. Miller, *The Contemplative Practitioner* and *Educating for Wisdom and Compassion*, categorize types, but other experts discuss ways that have worked for them as well. Rachel Kessler's *Soul of Education* is especially helpful as are Richard L. Graves and Donald R. Gallehr's essays in *The Spiritual Side of Writing*. Depending on the class and maturity of the student, I choose what I think best suits that group of students. Sometimes it is only fifteen minutes of silent time each day. Sometimes, I ask students to include mindfulness practice into parts of their day along with silent time. I often bring movement meditation into class or sound mediation that relies on a mantra.

As I get to know my students better and better, I let intuition guide me and I listen to them when they make requests. Students appreciate knowing about the various forms, because they seem to have a need for comparing forms. Once they begin to accept meditation as part of the class, they like to branch out and try other forms. I am happy also to write that it is becoming more common for some students to already practice meditation. These students usually ask me if they may continue their existing practice instead of beginning the one I am introducing to the group. Naturally, I say yes, because as I mentioned above, the goal is to live a contemplative life, not just to learn meditation practice.

I teach in a state university in sixteen-week semesters. Sixteen weeks is barely enough time to "start" a practice, let alone "understand" one. Moreover, the Western world today seems to want everything easy and fast, but meditation is not fast and the commitment to a daily practice can be a challenge.

In sixteen weeks, I can only hope that students will grow less resistant; that a few will continue meditation after the course is over; and that they will experience wonder, awe, and an epiphany or moment of grace as Dick Graves calls it. My students tend to be people "in" and "of" the world. I hope that in sixteen weeks they will reflect on the idea that people who live a contemplative life learn what it means to be "in" the world but not "of" the world. They live with values that denounce greed, violence, and waste, and they embrace values based on compassion, wisdom, and tolerance. They learn to "re-see" the world as well as their function in it. This new second sight is essential to writers, and it is essential to opening ourselves to the potential for wonder and awe evoked when spiritual learning occurs.

As students write and revise, I hope that their meditation practice leads them to second sight—not just of their writing but also of their daily lives. For all practical intents and purposes, meditation practice is a countercultural activity. It asks that they slow down, that they take a second (or third, or fourth, etc.) look, and that they go inward and trust what they feel and think. As Miller (2007) states, "Ultimately, the holistic curriculum lets us realize our deeper sense of self, our soul" (p. 14). Meditation is an essential first step, but it needs to be integrated with course content, multiple ways of learning, and student choice.

In today's educational climate, especially in public or state schools, testing dominates decision making and curricular design. Teacher autonomy is threatened by this, as is student choice. The Democratic School movement attempts to counteract this alarming trend and so do holistic approaches to learning. Multiple ways of learning, even though we acknowledge them in theory, are rarely considered, and students are mostly "assigned" content that leads them to higher test scores rather than to significant transformative learning.

The contemporary emphasis on test scores steadily erodes teacher and student empowerment. This can be offset, however, with a change to holistic approaches to learning. The holistic way embraces logical ways of learning but not as the dominant way. The holistic way leads from the inner spirit of the learner and connects the spirit to multiple ways of learning. Course content and the need for higher test scores do not have to be abandoned when switching to a holistic approach, but the drive to achieve higher test scores is subordinated to the joy and awe that arises out of transcendence.

Course content, combined with student choice and a holistic approach, can lead to transcendence, which leads to significant learning. Significant learning is supposed to be what test scores seek to demonstrate. Holistic educators believe that nonlinear ways of learning produce significant learning, and we stand committed to work that engages the learner holistically. We stand committed to the spirit of the learner and the learner's whole potential.

References

Gallehr, D. R. (1997). What is the sound of no hand writing? The use of secularized Zen koans in the teaching of writing. In R. P. Foehr & S. A. Schiller (Eds.), *The spiritual side of writing: Releasing the learner's whole potential* (pp. 95–104). Portsmouth, NH: Boynton/Cook.

Graves, R. L. (1997). Grace, in pedagogy. In R. P. Foehr & S. A. Schiller (Eds.), *The spiritual side of writing: Releasing the learner's whole potential* (pp. 15–24). Portsmouth, NH: Boynton/Cook.

Kessler, R. (2000). *The soul of education*. Alexandria, VA: Association for Supervision and Curriculum Development.

Miller, J. P. (1993). *Holistic teacher*. Toronto: Ontario Institute for Studies in Education Press.

Miller, J. P. (1994). *The contemplative practitioner: Mediation in education and the professions*. Toronto: Ontario Institute for Studies in Education Press.

Miller, J. P. (2006). *Educating for wisdom and compassion*. Thousand Oaks, CA: Corwin.

Miller, J. P. (2007). *The holistic curriculum*. 2nd ed. Toronto: Ontario Institute for Studies in Education Press.

Moffett, J. (1994). *The universal schoolhouse: Spiritual awakening through education*. San Francisco: Jossey-Bass.

Rocha, D. L. D. (2003). *Schools where children matter: Exploring educational alternatives*. Brandon, VT: Foundation for Educational Renewal.

CHAPTER FOUR

~

Sustaining Life

Education for Sustainability

Gary Babiuk

Holistic Nature of Education for Sustainability

An urgent concern for the world is how we humans will be able to sustain our existence here on beautiful planet earth amid all of the massive disturbances we have created in our ecosystems. Issues such as climate change, environment degradation, species extinction, and social upheaval including poverty, violence, and social injustices are threatening our very survival. We need to not only determine how to sustain life but also consider how we can thrive as a human species. We have to find a way to ensure our well-being now and for future generations.

As Ervin Laszlo states, "Evolving human spirit and consciousness is the first vital cause shared by the whole human family. . . . Each of us must start with ourselves to evolve our consciousness" (2009, p. 98). This consciousness includes thinking and acting with more sustainability. This problem for how we humans are impacting the natural world, Mother Earth, is not new. Over the last few decades, these concerns for how humans are affecting other forms of life and ecosystems on which we are dependent along with massive global social upheavals have resulted in a call for countries to develop programs for Education for Sustainable Development (ESD). This call for action has its roots in the earlier environmental movements.

The first part of this chapter explores the history and definitions of education for sustainability and outlines some of the actions being taken to move it forward. These actions not only are necessary to ensure human survival but also can lead to enhanced human well-being and be a source of joy. The second part presents a brief overview of education for sustainability and offers specific resources helpful to teachers.

Historical Roots

The historical roots of education for sustainability extend farther back than the 1960s when Rachel Carson wrote *Silent Spring*, which for many of us brought attention for the first time on the environment and the impact that humans were making on it. Carson's book and the subsequent development of environmental and "green" movements have their foundations in the early 1800s with the birth of science and biology outlined in the writings of Charles Lyell and Charles Darwin. There are also roots in the transcendentalists, especially Emerson and Thoreau, who influenced later social movements led by the likes of Gandhi and Martin Luther King. "Ecological authors, including John Muir, Grey Owl, Ernest Thompson Seaton, Aldo Leopold, and Rachel Carson, discussed issues of sustainability. Their concerns stem from the exponential growth of human population and the load placed on the natural environment" (Manitoba Education and Training, 2000, p. 51).

Since the 1970s, the United Nation has taken a lead in addressing the issues of human and environmental degradation. In 1972, at meetings in Stockholm, a declaration and action plan was developed to deal with issues around climate change, the influence of science and technology, and air and water pollution. Through subsequent meetings and commissions, the action plan was refined, and the concept of sustainable development was defined by the Brundtland Commission in 1987. Then in 1992, representatives of member countries of the United Nations met at a World Conference on Environment and Development in Rio de Janeiro and created a report that outlines the key role that education needs to play in "the advancement of a sustainable future."[1]

Through the rest of the 1990s, numerous international meetings recommended the need for education to play an active role in addressing issues of sustainability and development. "Governments should strive to update or prepare strategies aimed at integrating environment and development as a cross-cutting issue into education at all levels within the next three years" (Manitoba Education and Training, 2000, p. 53). This need to educate all humans has become even more urgent over the first decade of the twenty-first century as scientists consistently warn of the many disastrous consequents humans face if we do not address the causes of climate change. During this time, the definition of what is meant by Education for Sustainable Development or Education for Sustainability has been developed and debated.

Decade of Education for Sustainable Development

After years of discussion about what countries could do to bring about a sustainable ethic to human actions, the United Nations, through the United Nations Educational, Scientific and Cultural Organization (UNESCO), decided to declare a decade to develop and implement a strategy for ESD.

The United Nations Decade of Education for Sustainable Development (DESD) is a complex and far-reaching undertaking. The environmental, social, cultural, and economic implications are enormous and touch many aspects of life of the world's population. The overall goal of the DESD is to integrate the principles, values, and practices of sustainable development into all aspects of education and learning. This educational effort will encourage changes in behavior that will create a more sustainable future in terms of environmental integrity, economic viability, and a just society for present and future generations (UNESCO, 2008).

As a result, since 2005, countries around the world have been engaged in efforts to develop educational programs in formal (schools), informal (government departments, nongovernmental organizations [NGOs], business, etc.), and nonformal (general public) settings. Numerous international meetings have been held to assess the progress of the decade and encourage renewed efforts to educate not just school students but also all citizens about the urgency of these educational efforts to create a more sustainable world. There have been mixed results, with many suggesting that we have not moved far enough and that there is still much to be done.

Definition of Education for Sustainability

But what is education for sustainability? In his book *The Hidden Connections: A Science of Sustainable Living*, Fritjof Capra notes, on the origin of the concept of sustainability,

> The concept of sustainability was introduced in the early 1980s by Lester Brown, founder of the Worldwatch Institute, who defined a sustainable society as one that is able to satisfy its needs without diminishing the chances of future generations. Several years later, the report of the World Commission on Environment and Development (the "Brundtland Report") used the same definition to present the notion of sustainable development: "Humankind has the ability to achieve sustainable development—to meet the needs of the present without compromising the ability of future generations to meet their own needs." (2002, p. 229)

This definition points to the fact that sustainability is more than just about the environment; it is a multistrand concept that includes the natural world and the social and economic aspects all linked to basic human needs. As Rosalyn McKeown further makes clear, "Sustainable development has three components: environment, society, and economy. If you consider the three to be overlapping circles of the same size, the area of overlap in the center is human well-being. As the environment, society, and economy become more aligned, the area of overlap increases, and so does human well-being" (2006, p. 11).

In fact some would suggest that the three areas are nested into each other with the environment being the largest, human society nested into it, and the economy much smaller nested into the human society, an indication that we need to consider the environment in all of our human decisions.

There is an even more succinct way of defining sustainability, and it is reported to have been suggested by an African delegate at a UNESCO meeting. It states that sustainability is "Enough, for All, Forever." This again highlights the three components of sustainability: we need an equitable and sufficient quality of life, for everyone on the planet, including the generations to come. This certainly matches the First Nations ideal of the "seventh generation principle," also known as the "precautionary principle," which guides us to consider future generations in all our decisions about how we will affect Mother Earth.[2]

All of these statements seem to be moving away from a primary focus on the environment, or the environment and the economy (development), instead focusing on an integration of both of these with the human or cultural aspect of sustainability. They are putting forth the concept of sustainability not just in an economic sense but also in terms of the human conditions such as health and well-being, arts and culture, safety, and education. The use of the term Education for Sustainability (EfS) rather than Education for Sustainable Development (ESD) also helps move our thinking away from just the economic and environmental focus, to which the word development seems to refer, and helps us consider the interconnection of all three aspects.

ESD as a Values Issue

Sustainability is *not* a problem of planet earth. Whatever we humans do, earth will continue to evolve, as it has done over billions of years, at times inhabitable to life but, in most recent times, home to humans. Thus, "*The problem of sustainability is a human values problem*, because sustainability is about sustaining something, and what that 'something' is is (at least in its major part) a matter of human choice based on values" (Babiuk & Falkenberg, 2010, p. 9). Humans must satisfy their needs but without hindering our future generations' ability to satisfy theirs. As I and Thomas Falkenberg have suggested earlier,

> What a society's needs are—maybe with the exception of basic survival needs—is a matter of societal values. The problem of sustainability, then, is *the problem of creating and sustaining the conditions for a particular way of human living for the current generation and future generations.* Thus, *the problem of sustainability is a human, a value, and a responsibility problem* (responsibility toward future generations). (2010, p. 9)

Holistic Nature of EfS

The movement toward Education for Sustainability is holistic. The basic holistic principles of balance, inclusion, and connection as outlined by John P. Miller (2008) are being played out in the development of this ideal over the last decade. The balance has occurred as we move away from just an environmental, "green" focus to seeing sustainable education as including the socioeconomic and the sociocultural as well. All are important and need to be in balance to provide for human well-being and a quality of life on the planet that honors all living beings.

The inclusion principle is exemplified in the bringing together of many more voices into the discussion of sustainability in general and education in particular. The conversation has widened to include not just those in education and government but also members of other professions, community groups, NGOs, and businesses. Education for Sustainability is now being seen as essential for the future well-being of individuals, communities, and the globe.

The connection aspect of holistic education is illustrated in the interconnecting of traditionally separate disciplines, subjects, and knowledge into an integrated whole. This mirrors the earth systems that are interconnected at a physical or environmental level and also at a human level. The environmental issues of pollution and land degradation and the economic issues of resource depletion and globalization are now being considered with the human issues of social injustice, poverty, violence, and racial and gender inequalities. This connection can be seen in the groups that are now talking, thinking, planning, and acting together to solve these very complex and systemic problems.

A book that outlines this wider social interconnection is *Blessed Unrest*, by Paul Hawken, which explores "the movement" with no name or leader that is very exciting.[3] Hawken, an environmentalist, entrepreneur, and author, is one of the founders that have "created a hub for global civil society

(WiseEarth.org) providing an open-source networking platform that links NGOs (non-governmental organizations), funders, business, government, social entrepreneurs, students, organizations, academics, activists, scientists, and citizens" (Strand, 2008, p. 58). This connectedness is fundamental to humanity solving the global issues that face us, and as Hawken states,

> when we truly see ourselves we see that we are connected to all else, that we are inseparable from every molecule, thought, child, twig, and creature on earth. When we know that to take care of one life we have to take care of all life, and that life includes what we say, how we act, what we do, and what we honor, that is the beginning of the sacred embodiment that leads to true civilization. (Strand, 2008, p. 59)

This understanding of the balance, inclusion, and interconnectedness is necessary for our world to move sustainably into the future. Education for Sustainability is the movement we need in education that will allow us to develop the knowledge, skills, and values together with our children to envision and create this "true civilization."

Key Characteristics of Education for Sustainability
In a document produced by UNESCO at the beginning of the Decade for ESD, the key characteristics of education where outlined. These characteristics are as follows:

1. Interdisciplinary and holistic: learning for sustainable development embedded in the whole curriculum, not as a separate subject;
2. Values driven: it is critical that the assumed norms—the shared values and principles underpinning sustainable development—are made explicit so that that can be examined, debated, tested, and applied;
3. Critical thinking and problem solving: leading to confidence in addressing the dilemmas and challenges of sustainable development;
4. Multi-methods: word, art, drama, debate, experience, . . . different pedagogies which model the process. Teaching that is geared simply to passing on knowledge should be recast into an approach in which teachers and learners work together to acquire knowledge and play a role in shaping the environment in their educational institutions;
5. Participatory decision making: learners participate in decisions on how they are to learn;
6. Locally relevant: addressing local as well as global issues, and using the language(s) which learners most commonly use. Concept of sustain-

able development must be carefully expressed in other languages—languages and cultures say things differently, and each language has creative ways of expressing new concepts. (UNESCO, 2005, p. 18)

Sustainable Well-Being

Another aspect of sustainability is the notion of "human well-being" and quality of life. This again moves our thinking of sustainability away from just the environment to consider how humans will live on the earth. Certainly the health of the environment, Mother Earth, is key to our survival, but within this care of earth, how can we as humans live well. The Millennium Ecosystem Assessment identifies five aspects of human well-being:

- *security*: personal safety, secure resource access
- *basic material for good life*: adequate livelihoods, sufficient nutritious food, shelter, access to goods
- *health*: strength, feeling well, access to clean air and water
- *good social relations*: social cohesion, mutual respect, ability to help others
- *freedom of choice and action*: opportunity to be able to achieve what an individual values doing and being (Hassan, Scholes, & Ash, 2005, p. 28)

There are other indexes such as the Canadian Index of Well-being; the Happy Planet Index, developed by the New Economics Foundation; and the Friends of the Earth and the Gross National Happiness used by the Government of Bhutan. All of these are moving away from using just the economic indicators such as GNP or GDP or per capita income as indicators of the health and well-being of people, societies, and earth. We need other ways to measure human well-being.

Many other authors, educators, and leaders have outlined how we can go about transforming our human societies into sustainable ones for our future well-being. Duane Elgin (2010) suggests in his book *Voluntary Simplicity: Toward a Way of Life That Is Outwardly Simple, Inwardly Rich* that we cannot continue on the current path of destruction but must swiftly and voluntarily choose a different path, one based on living on the earth more lightly. He suggests that simplicity is not sacrifice but a way of living that fulfills our basic needs and well-being and, at the same time, addresses the issues of peak oil, climate change, overpopulations, and species extinction. He also outlines that simplicity does not mean living in poverty, or that we all have to embrace rural living, ugly living, or economic stagnation. He states,

> The circle has closed. The Earth is a single system and we humans have reached beyond its regenerative capacity. It is of the highest urgency that we invent new ways of living that are sustainable. The starting gun of history has already gone off and the time for creative action has arrived. With lifestyles of conscious simplicity, we can seek our riches in caring families and friendships, reverence for nature, meaningful work, exuberant play, social contribution, collaboration across generations, local community, and creative arts. With conscious simplicity, we can seek lives that are rich with experiences, satisfaction, and learning rather than packed with things. With these new ingredients in the lives of our civilizations, we can redefine progress, awaken a new social consciousness, and establish a realistic foundation for a sustainable and promising future. (pp. 23–24)

With this statement, Elgin suggests that we can bring about change in our living right now that will lead to a more sustainable world and future. We can make the change without sacrificing our well-being and happiness.

Another interesting group who have completed extensive research into human well-being is the New Economics Foundation (NEF). Their review of the most up-to-date data distilled the following five ways to well-being that we should include in our day-to-day lives. They include the following:

- Connect . . . With the people around you. With family, friends, colleagues and neighbours, At home, work, school or in your local community. Think of these as the cornerstones of your life and invest time in developing them. Building these connections will support and enrich you every day.
- Be active . . . Go for a walk or run. Step outside. Cycle. Play a game. Garden. Dance. Exercising makes you feel good. Most importantly, discover a physical activity you enjoy and that suits your level of mobility and fitness.
- Take notice . . . Be curious. Catch sight of the beautiful. Remark on the unusual. Notice the changing seasons. Savour the moment, whether you are walking to work, eating lunch or talking to friends. Be aware of the work around you and what you are feeling. Reflecting on your experiences will help you appreciate what matters to you.
- Keep learning . . . Try something new. Rediscover an old interest. Sign up for that course. Take on a different responsibility at work. Fix a bike. Learn to play an instrument or how to cook your favourite food. Set a

challenge you will enjoy achieving. Learning new things will make you more confident as well as being fun.
- Give . . . Do something nice for a friend, or a stranger. Thanks someone. Smile. Volunteer your time. Join a community group. Look out, as well as in. Seeing yourself, and your happiness, linked to the wider community can be incredibly rewarding and creates connections with the people around you. (Thompson et al., 2008, p. iii).

These actions are not complicated! In fact, they are ones most of us already do on a regular basis. Thus, if we consider that we can in fact live more sustainably and enhance our well-being without increasing our ecological footprint on the planet or even reducing it, we can see that we can in fact make a difference and move to a more sustainable life.

Ways of Approaching Education for Sustainability
With the challenges of addressing the sustainability issues we currently face, there have been a multitude of actions suggested on how we educate ourselves to understand and act to solve sustainability issues. Let me offer a brief overview of some that seem very promising.

The Center for EcoLiteracy (www.ecoliteracy.org), whose directors include such important educators and thinkers in the field of sustainability as David Orr, Fritjof Capra, and Zenobia Barlow, is a strong voice for education of sustainability, and the center provides professional development opportunities and publications. In one of their recent publications, *EcoLiterate: How Educators Are Cultivating Emotional, Social, and Ecological Intelligence* (Goleman, Bennett, & Barlow, 2012), five practices are outlined that "have the profound capacity to help create and sustain healthier relationships with other people and the planet" (p. 12).

The five practices are as follows:

1. Developing empathy for all forms of life,
2. Embracing sustainability as a community,
3. Making the invisible visible,
4. Anticipating unintended consequences, and
5. Understanding how nature sustains life. (pp. 10–17)

This book is a guide for professional development as it includes case studies, website supports, and professional development strategies to engage collegial discussion, professional reflection, and action. Basing our teaching around these five principles can help students become ecoliterate. Students become more critical in their thinking and inquiry and come to be more sustainable decision makers.

Another important educational organization that provides insights into education for sustainability is the Institute for Humane Education. The cofounder, Zoe Weil has written a book, *Most Good, Least Harm: A Simple Principle for a Better World and Meaningful Life* (2009). She outlines the principles to use and practice for us to "examine the challenges facing our planet—from human oppression, to environmental degradation, to animal cruelty, to escalating materialism—and invites people to live intentional, examined, and meaningful lives that solve the problems we face" (p. 3). The principles she suggests are as follows:

1. Providing accurate information about the issues of our time so that people have the information they need to confront challenges,
2. Fostering the 3 Cs: Curiosity, Creativity, and Critical thinking so that people have the skills to meet challenges,
3. Instilling the 3 Rs: Reverence, Respect, and Responsibility, so that people have the motivation to face challenges,
4. Offering positive choices and tools for problem solving, so that people are empowered to make healthy decisions for themselves and the world, and solve challenges, and finally
5. You will need to actively and consciously cultivate what I call the 3 Is: Inquiry, Introspection, and Integrity. (Weil, 2009, pp. 3–10)

Through a process outlined in the Weil book, we can examine our own thinking and actions in relation to sustainability and the "most good, least harm" principle. Weil's book along with the resources and professional development opportunities found at the Institute for Humane Education (www.HumaneEducation.org) can guide educators and students alike in examining their current lifestyle and consumer decisions in order to bring sustainable well-being into one's life.

Educational Resources for Sustainable Approaches in Teaching

Writing about and for sustainability is holistic and integrative as is the understanding of it. Systems thinking, seeing the connections between all things, is a fundamental way of perceiving the world; one sees the universe as holistic. It is about observing and listening to the world around us. It is about making the invisible visible. It is about connecting to the natural world, which is not just wild places but life in urban spaces as well. It is in understanding that we *are* nature, not separate from it, and through being mindful of our connection to the natural systems of air, water, and soil, we can create an empathy for the natural order and a deep understanding of how nature sustains life. Systems thinking is not only about the environment but also about social justice, equity, and human well-being. It is about introspection in order to help us see our role in creating the problems and taking action to solve them. Joyful writing can help us express this understanding.

Sustainability has many topics to focus writing. They could be in the areas of social justice such as poverty, equity issues, violence, women's rights, energy use, and waste management, or in environmental issues such as air, water, and soil degradation, sometimes referred to as our "ecological footprint." The topics could also be in the areas where advances are being made to improve the environment and social condition, sometimes referred to as our "ecological handprint." Furthermore, There are many reasons we write: for work, for pleasure, for communication, and much more. How and why we write to enhance our sustainable living is also varied, but none of them are isolated in themselves. They all connect to each other and support and lead to each other. A few reasons for why we write and the ways they promote sustainability and holistic connections are listed below for consideration.

1. Contemplation: We sometimes use writing for contemplation; journaling may be one way in which we write "to just be." It is a writing process that makes tangible what is normally elusive—as an important avenue for personal and professional development. Journaling, as a writing process, is often confused with keeping a diary or simple logging of events. These are fine in their own right, but the goal of journaling can also be to enhance one's sense of well-being by clarifying vague thoughts and elusive feelings. Thoughts and feelings become more concrete when we not only "think" them but also write, read, and respond to them. Often, writing down thoughts and feelings enhances our ability to sort out what is truly meaningful and assists us in gaining perspective on the behavior changes we are experiencing or trying to make. Further, if we document (and date) experienced thoughts and feelings, we can see over time the development of new perspectives and behavior changes. Writing also suggests a permanence through which commitment to change is enhanced; as well it enhances one's thought-feeling reaction to life experiences. Since the writing process is private unless one chooses to share it, we can be totally frank as we write.

2. Inspirational: This kind of writing may arise out of contemplation writing and lead to creative activity and action. It can be in the form

of poetry or stories. Many writers committed to social action such as Gandhi, Martin Luther King, and Nelson Mandela have provided such writing to the world. Authors such Aldo Leopold, Henry David Thoreau, and Rachel Carson have done the same kind of inspirational writing on behalf of the environment. We can add to this body of writing with our own heartfelt, soulful, and spirited writing.

3. Aspirational: This writing leads to making commitments or plans to take action on behalf of a sustainability cause. It is usually the first step to sustainably transforming our life and community. It puts our wishes into concrete written word. This writing is usually born out of contemplation and inspiration.
4. Informational: This kind of writing is usually based on some compiling of information or research. It helps us clarify the issues, provides insights into the problem, and may also outline some possible courses of action. It usually occurs after we are interested in an issue and before we plan to take action.
5. Call for action or protest: This writing puts into words what needs to be done and why. It calls on us to stand up and let our voices be heard for a cause that may be social or environmental. It is usually meant to encourage others to join you in some sustainable cause or action.
6. Historical writing: Here we try to record what has happened in our efforts to transform the world. It records our successes, failures, and challenges to help inform future action.

All of these forms of writing are necessary for moving us along toward a sustainable future. They can take the form of poems, essays, letters, narratives, expositions, editorials, and so forth. If we engage in writing in a group setting, where we share ideas and concerns, then our commitment to transformational action can be even more powerful. All of these forms of writing tend to build on each other and provide the information, emotional, and spiritual energy needed in our desire to transform the world from one that is on a path of destruction to one in which we can begin to take action and change our values and behaviors to honor other humans and the earth itself.

It is also helpful to be aware of the many excellent resources out there and examples of writing projects, some of them embedded in the curriculum, or lessons that focus on sustainability issues. These resources are only meant as a starting point and are not considered all encompassing, for there are far more resources than can be included in this chapter. The following are a few examples of how joyful writing in the area of these topics can encourage all of us to lead more sustainable lives and enhance our well-being.

- The UNESCO Education for Sustainable Development website provides an overview of what is going on at a global level. It is a good starting point for your inquiry into Education for Sustainability. Access it at www.unesco.org.
- UNESCO—Teaching and Learning for a Sustainable Future: This is an excellent online, interactive, multimedia teacher education program. It has individual modules that help you explore and learn about a multitude of topics. It has an Across the Curriculum section, a Contemporary Issues section, including a subtopic on Indigenous Knowledge and Sustainability, and a section on Teaching and Learning Strategies. It is very comprehensive and will provide numerous writing activities on many topics and issues. It is one of the top web resources when it comes to Education for Sustainable Development. Access the site at www.unesco.org.
- Just as the Charter of Human Rights outlines the principles for social interaction, the Earth Charter outlines the interdependent principles for a sustainable way of life as a common standard by which the conduct of all individuals, organizations, businesses, governments, and transnational institutions is to be guided and assessed. The principles are organized under Respect and Care for the Community of Life, Ecological Integrity, Social and Economic Justice, and Democracy, Nonviolence, and Peace. It can be accessed at www.earthcharterinaction.org/invent/images/uploads/echarter_english.pdf.

Learning for a Sustainable Future—Connecting the Dots: The website for the group Learning for a Sustainable Future (www.lsf-lst.ca/en) has been developed to present resources, curriculum, and lessons for Education for Sustainability. These resources are based on environmental and social action. The projects and resources are multidisciplinary and include writing activities in all projects. One particular section, Connecting the Dots, is very helpful as it is organized around the following seven strategies:

1. Learning locally—community as classroom,
2. Integrated learning,
3. Acting on learning,
4. Real-world connections,
5. Considering alternative perspectives,
6. Inquiry, and
7. Sharing responsibility for learning with students.

8. All in all, this is a very helpful site for teaching about sustainability, with most documents downloadable.

- Partnership Education in Action: This resource publication edited by Dierdre Bucciarelli and Sarah Pirtle for the Center for Partnership Studies in collaboration with the Foundation for Educational Renewal is a full curriculum outline to address the issues of gender inequality that Riane Eisler has outlined in her other books, *The Chalice and the Blade* and *Tomorrow's Children*. This curriculum is full of units and lessons that address the issues of inequality through activities that are social studies and language arts oriented but integrated with the creative arts. It is a complete guide to not only developing curriculum but also transforming a school culture based on a partnership worldview, in which we think and act in a way that honors "a more democratic and egalitarian family and social structure, gender equality, a low level of institutional violence and abuse . . . and a system of beliefs, stories and values that supports and validates this kind of structure as normal and right" (Eisler, 2000, p. 5). *The Partnership Education in Action* publication is full of writing activities that would allow students to explore issues of social injustices, which are also a crucial aspect of Education for Sustainability.
- The Manitoba Education, Citizenship and Youth Department website provides an overview of the curriculum development of a province that has been working on this initiative since 2000. It outlines curriculum ideas and resources. Although it is focused on Manitoba, there are many links to national and international resources and programs. Access their website at www.edu.gov.mb.ca.
- The Wiserearth website is an interesting and action-oriented one. It is a social network for sustainability. There are thousands of groups connecting to other like-minded groups and lots of news of exciting projects from around the world. It certainly is on the cusp of future orientated global action. It is worth a look and may be accessed at www.wiserearth.org.
- *Global Forest*: This little book is a real gem of storytelling and inspiration. The narratives are all based on scientific research but are told in a personal voice, with intriguing insights and wisdom being at the heart of each story. Diane Beresford-Kroeger is a botanist and medical biochemist who is an expert on medical, environmental, and nutritional properties of trees, but her stories about the forest ecosystems weave the scientific perspective into ancient knowing. They are enlightening

and joyful but also cautionary about how we are endangering the very ecosystems that have provided humans with food, clothing, shelter, and medicine for thousands of years. This would be a great resource for encouraging students to write their own stories about the natural systems in which they are interested. It is also just a good read and inspirational storytelling.

- Edward Burtynsky's photographic works (www.edwardburtynsky.com): This is an awesome site. It houses a set of photographic images from around the world that Burtynsky has used to show how humans have altered the natural world. He has basically made the invisible visible and shown us what is hidden from view in our overconsumptive society. His photographs show how we have wrought destruction to the earth because of our unquenchable desire for oil to run our cars and heat and cool our homes and offices and our never-ending desire to have the latest in consumer products, particularly electronic devices. He has taken photos in China at large manufacturing sites and at polluted areas where "ewaste" is being recycled at tremendous human suffering. In North America, he has photographed oil drilling, tire waste yards, plane graveyards that expand for thousands of acres, mining quarries, tailing yards, oil sands, and massive highway turnpikes. In India, he has captured photos of the coastline where old oil tankers are being dismantled by manual labor without protection from the oil still remaining in the hulls. There are many more images that will be both breathtaking in their artistic beauty but at the same time shocking to the degree of destruction. It will move you and should make you think next time you go to the store to buy something or fill up your car with gas. This site will provide an excellent resource for students to write about their impressions of the photos, investigate them further, and reflect how their reactions might lead to some sustainable action both personally and as a community. If anything it is worth a look to quench your curiosity. There are also some other resources included on the website such as video clips and introduction to the award-winning documentary *Manufactured Landscapes* that follows Burtynsky as he is taking photos in China. Again you must see these amazing photos.
- *Creative Journey through Journaling*: Julie Cameron has published a number of other books that build on *The Artist's Way* (1992) and outline additional tools and exercises to enhance creativity. They are *The Vein of Gold: A Journey to Your Creative Heart* (1996) and *Walking in This World: The Practical Art of Creativity* (2002).

The book *Smart by Nature: Schooling for Sustainability* is based on the Guiding Principles for Sustainable Schooling:

1. Nature is our teacher,
2. Sustainability is a community practice,
3. The real world is the optimal learning environment, and
4. Sustainable living is rooted in a deep knowledge of place.

Most of the book provides stories about schools from across the United States that have developed a sustainable culture, gardens, food programs, and redesigned buildings. It would be an excellent resource for students to be inspired and write their own stories of making sustainable changes to their classroom, schools, courtyards, and outdoor fields that surround the school. See the website for the Center for Ecoliteracy for more resources at www.ecoliteracy.org.

Conclusion

This brief overview of education for sustainability is meant to help the reader see that we need to take a sustainable stance in our lives and work. "Creating a sustainable world is feasible—in principle. Creating it in practice depends on what we do today: whether we evolve our consciousness, and begin to change consciously and in time" (Laszlo, 2009, p. 90). We believe that writing in all its forms, along with the other creative arts, is a fundamental way of expressing that humans need to transform their action in order to make the consciousness shift to live as if earth matters. Writing will provide each of us a way to connect to our inner life, deepen our connection to our family and community, and become a caring member of a sustainable global village. Holistic writing activities can be found throughout *Sustaining the Writing Spirit*, but one more specific to sustainability is found in chapter 20, "Writing the Outdoors: Three Days in Nature."

The process of joyful writing in the name of sustainable well-being is as varied as the forms of writing. The topics are not unique but have an urgent aspect to them. We as a human species cannot wait much longer to take action to transform our world from one focused on consumerism, aggression, and greed to one of voluntary simplicity, peace, and caring. We need to act now, and writing can be one of many ways that our voices for transformation of our world into one that is sustainable for generations to come can be heard.

Notes

1. This meeting was held again in Rio de Janeiro in 2012 and was called "Rio+20." At the conclusion of this meeting, much had been discussed, but there has been limited movement on education for sustainable development across the globe in the twenty years since the first meeting.

2. The term "First Nations" is used in Canada to identify the many aboriginal tribes and nations that are found across the provinces and territories. It does not include the Inuit (northern aboriginal peoples) and Metis (people of mixed aboriginal and European ancestry).

3. Paul Hawken is the author of several books that explore aspects of sustainability. They include *The Next Economy* (1983), *The Ecology of Commerce: A Declaration of Sustainability* (1993), *Natural Capitalism: Creating the Next Industrial Revolution* (1999), and *Blessed Unrest: How the Largest Movement in the World Came into Being and Why No One Saw It Coming* (2007).

References

Babiuk, G., & Falkenberg, T. (2010). *Sustainable development and living through changing teacher education and teaching in Manitoba*. Winnipeg, Canada: Manitoba Education and Canadian Council on Learning.

Beresford-Kroeger, D. (2010). *The global forest*. Toronto: Viking.

Bucciarelli, D., & Pirtle, S. (Eds.). (2001). *Partnership education in action*. Tucson, AZ: Center for Partnership Studies.

Cameron, J. (1992). *The artist's way: A spiritual path to higher creativity*. New York: Tarcher Putnam.

Capra, F. (2002). *The hidden connections: A science of sustainable living*. New York: Anchor.

Eisler, R. (2000). *Tomorrow's children: A blueprint for partnership education in the twenty-first century*. Boulder, CO: Westview.

Elgin, D. (2010). *Voluntary simplicity: Toward a way of life that is outwardly simple, inwardly rich*. New York: Harper.

Goleman, D., Bennett, L., & Barlow, Z. (2012). *EcoLiterate: How educators are cultivating emotional, social, and ecological literacy*. San Francisco: Jossey-Bass.

Hassan, R., Scholes, R., & Ash, N. (Eds.). (2005). *Ecosystems and human well-being: Current state and trends*. Millennium Ecosystem Assessment Series 1. Washington, DC: Island Press. Retrieved from www.millenniumassessment.org/documents/document.766.aspx.pdf.

Laszlo, E. (2009). *Worldshift 2012: Making green business, new politics, and higher consciousness work together*. Toronto: McArthur.

Manitoba Education and Training, School Division. (2000). *Education for sustainable future: A resource for curriculum developers, teachers, and administrators*. Winnipeg, Canada: Author.

McKeown, R. (with Hopkins, C., Rizzin, R., & Chrystalbridge, M.). (2006). *Education for sustainable development toolkit*. Paris: UNESCO, Section for Education for Sustainable Development. Retrieved from www.esdtoolkit.org/.

Miller, J. P. (2008). *The holistic curriculum* (2nd ed.). Toronto: University of Toronto Press.

Stone, M. K. (2009). *Smart by nature: Schooling for sustainability*. Berkeley, CA: Center for Ecoliteracy.

Strand, C. (2008, fall). The movement with no name. *Buddhist Review, Tricycle*, pp. 58–61.

Thompson, S., Aked, J., Marks, N., & Cordon, C. (2008, October 21). Five ways to well-being: The evidence. Centre for Well-Being, New Economics Foundation. Retrieved from www.neweconomics.org/.

United Nations Educational, Scientific and Cultural Organization (UNESCO). (2005). United Nations decade of education for sustainable development 2005–2014: Draft international implementation scheme. Retrieved from http://unesdoc.unesco.org/images/0013/001399/139937e.pdf.

UNESCO. (2008). Education for sustainable development (ESD). Retrieved from www.unesco.org/.

Weil, Z. (2009). *Most good, least harm: A simple principle for a better world and meaningful life*. New York: Astria.

CHAPTER FIVE

Contemplating Great Things in Soul and Place

- *Overview*: Participants view photographs of beautiful places, write a reflective response, and share with others.[1] A process using movement to and from inner and exterior spaces and silence creates an atmosphere that encourages analysis, reflection, and creativity.
- *Materials*: Photographs or postcards of beautiful places, paper or journal notebook, and a pencil or pen.
- *Suggested time*: Ninety-minute minimum, can be extended.
- *Participants*: At least two people are needed for this activity.
- *Types of learning*: Visual, verbal (written and spoken), physical, intellectual, emotional, spiritual, social, environmental, and reflective.
- *Rhetorical forms*: Prose and poetry.
- *Prerequisite* (optional): Knowledge of poetic forms.

This holistic writing activity allows people to create a poem, write a reflective response, and share with others. It strengthens relationships with soil, soul, and society. At its core we find the soul; we find transformation as an ontological phenomenon of infinite capacity. This phenomenon can open us to the power we hold within to shape and live our lives. We learn to see that the inner and outer rhythms that shape life can be used for our benefit and growth. More importantly, we also learn that, once demystified, the transformative power of soul can be accessible to us whenever we need it. We can understand, and share, the transformative power of soul as a skill to use when we shape relationships with one another and with our world.

The activity below integrates mind, body, and soul in a process of harmonious interconnections between images, words, silence, and creativity. Images, words, and silence are used repeatedly to initiate a movement from outer to inner and back again. This "is a basic human rhythm" that I also consider as a practical gateway leading to creativity and transformation (Bernie Neville, quoted in Kessler, 2000, p. 56).

Participants are asked to express the inner by creating their own poem about the greatness they have been able to newly see. Rachael Kessler informs us that "when creativity breaks through . . . mind, body, heart and spirit come together to spark the passion that fuels the motivation to learn to contribute and to savor our infinite capacity for growth" (2000, p. 114). When people share their creations at the end of the writing process, the capacity for growth is proclaimed and witnessed within the community. This validates their soul. In this context, soul refers to the inner depths from which feeling, knowledge, and change originate.

This process further creates the potential for participants to understand that greatness is accessible to us at any time if we allow the soul to transform our vision and to see that great things help our soul to emerge. While the outer shell of the process is linear, activities within each step are not; they awaken the participants to infinite opportunities for seeing greatness in soul and place. The relationship between linear and nonlinear ways of learning is created and allowed to flow. Ultimately, participants learn that greatness is everywhere if we just let our soul feel and see it, and that the soul itself is a transformative power that we can access in order to resee the world.

Balance, inclusion, and connection, so vital to holistic learning (Miller, 1996, p. 3), are maintained as they lead us to see that the transformative power of the soul can be studied as a phenomenon. As a phenomenon, this power can be sought; it does not need to remain a mystery. Our soul, then, becomes a paramount and practical place of growth of infinite learning.

The Activity

- Step 1: Two to five minutes of contemplating place as depicted in photos of Austria, the Czech Republic, and Hungary (poetic image)
- Step 2: Five- to ten-minute silent meditation (reverie and imagination)
- Step 3: Five- to ten-minute journal write on the greatness within these images of place (linguistic experience: connecting soul to place; combining mind and soul)
- Step 4: Five-minute scrutiny of potential greatness in the place where the workshop is held (poetic image)

- Step 5: Five- to ten-minute silent meditation (reverie and imagination)
- Step 6: Five- to ten-minute journal write on the greatness in the workshop place (linguistic experience: combining mind and soul)
- Step 7: Time for writing a poem about place and self (creative, imaginative, imagistic, and linguistic experience)
- Step 8: Discussion (linguistic connections to community: great things within and without)

In step 1, photographs of indoor and outdoor European scenes offer a poetic image as a starting point for imagination. Although I find these foreign shots to be effective, primarily because they are unfamiliar and uncommon, any photograph of beauty or the unfamiliar would work as well. These photos become the "poetic image," as Gaston Bachelard (1969) describes it, and they function as an externally located "great thing" that initiates the subsequent process. I ask students to contemplate the image and to imagine where the greatness exists in such a place.

The subsequent process combines imagination, the poetic image as great thing, and reverie about the great thing; participants are led to transforming the way they view place and self and then ultimately to seeing the transforming power of soul. They are transformed when they see that the transforming power of soul is primarily an internal event of viewpoint but is also a phenomenon within them that they can call forth at will.

Silent meditation is a natural choice to enhance or deepen the quality of reverie. In the silent space of meditation, soul and mind can mingle; imagination can freely move in a state of reverie and without the restraints of order or structure. The reverie that step 2 permits is natural and inevitable because, according to Bachelard, we cannot respond to the poetic image without a certain amount of reverie. For some people, particularly those who do not practice meditation, this activity can seem unfamiliar; five minutes of silent meditation feels extensive. Yet, for those who do practice meditation, five minutes may feel insufficient. Regardless of previous experience, however, each participant is likely to experience "a rest for the nervous system, a respite from the demands of others, and a chance to visit one's own inner life" (Kessler, 2000, p. 38).

The journal write in step 3 returns the participants to prose, a linguistic activity that is familiar and offers a time for personal, yet private, expression. It brings participants back to the outer, and as such it offers a bit of pseudo-closure that is calming. It also extends the intellectual reflection on place and self. The calming effect of this familiar linguistic activity helps to ready participants for the next step, which can be quite disarming for a number of reasons depending on the immediate environment.

In step 4, participants are asked to look for the greatness in the room they are in. As many of us know, classroom space can lack beauty. I generally find myself teaching in rooms made of painted beige cinderblock. Usually there is little daylight; shades are drawn and florescent lighting bears down unmercifully. Conference rooms are not much better either; chairs, tables, and perhaps audiovisual equipment are standard décor.

Creative tension arises when participants are asked to do something that at first seems illogical or impossible. Parker Palmer says, "Awareness is always heightened when we are caught in a creative tension" (1998, p. 74). At first, participants react with surprise, thinking there is nothing great to be found in such space, but then their perception takes a noticeable shift.

As a facilitator for the process, I have been able to observe the way people suddenly acquire new vision when looking about the room. Some of them walk about to discover different vantage points for vision. I have seen people touch and even smell wallpaper or painted walls. The more inquisitive might even crawl under a table and take a look from that point or sit on the floor instead of in a chair. This kind of exploration is encouraged by me. I often suggest using movement at this step in the activity as a means to see differently and as a means for knowing through the body. This step moves the participant into a deeper imaginative event that extends and further develops the potential for transformation.

Step 5 calls for additional reverie. It allows space for the imagination to again move toward transformation. The reverie in this step may actually be deeper because it may not feel as unfamiliar as it did earlier. Participants should be more relaxed at this stage. This is important, because "when a relaxed spirit meditates and dreams [as we hope they are doing during this step], immensity seems to expect images of immensity. The mind sees and continues to see objects, while the spirit finds the nest of immensity in an object" (Bachelard, 1969, p. 190). As one might assume, it is especially helpful at this point to extend the time for silent meditation. Even with people new to meditation or silence, I try to allow the full ten minutes. With more experienced participants, fifteen minutes is even more desirable.

With this extended time, people are more likely to see the poetic image within the space around them *and* see that the soul shapes what we see. Bachelard says, "We are obliged to acknowledge that poetry is a commitment of the soul. A consciousness of the soul is more relaxed, less intentionalized than a consciousness associated with the phenomena of the mind" (1969, p. xvii). In a meditative silent state, participants, when engaged with a poetic image, begin from a relaxed position, and the mind is less restricted. The soul can rise up and emerge. Then, its ability to shape the way we view our world can be recognized.

At this point, participants should "realize within [themselves] the pure being of pure imagination" (Bachelard, 1969, p. 184). They might also reach a more holistic view seeing that "the gifts of silence are intertwined; they cannot really be separated into cognitive, psychological, physiological, or spiritual" (Kessler, 2000, p. 43).

After the silent meditative reverie, participants are asked to return to journal writing in step 6. While it returns them to a familiar feeling and condition, it also is a prewriting activity for step 7. It is a stress-free way of releasing insights and realizations experienced during step 5. I don't allow very much time for this journal writing—ten minutes at the most. Sometimes, though, people want more time for this. They seem to be flowing over with ideas and language, and they want to let them out. I take this as evidence of what Palmer calls "the power of the living subject" (1998, p. 103). He says that "when we make the subject the center of our attention, we give it the respect and authority that we normally give only to human beings. We give it ontological significance (p. 103).

Furthermore, Bachelard says, "The communicability of an unusual image is a fact of great ontological significance" (1969, p. xiii). This ontological energy further primes them for creative expression in step 7 because its dynamism can take shape in the poetic image. In this way, participants are dealing with the nature of being, reality, and ultimate substance.

Step 7 asks that participants write a poem about the greatness in place and self. By writing a poem, participants are taking space, their position in and view of it, and using it as an act of expansion. Bachelard states, "Whatever affectivity that colors a given space, whether sad or ponderous, once it is poetically expressed, the sadness is diminished, the ponderousness lightened. Poetic space, because it is expressed, assumes values of expansion" (1969, p. 201). Through creativity and expansion, participants experience a new awareness and open themselves to the transforming power of soul. They learn, as Palmer tells us, that great things "are the irreducible elements of life itself" (1998, p. 109). They also learn that to see great things we must turn inward to the soul and let it guide our vision.

It is essential to allow sharing time to close the activity in step 8. Facilitators can invite participants to read their poetry, share their emotions experienced throughout, ask questions, and or give feedback or suggestions for changes in the process. The invitation must be sincere. Some people may not want to read their poem if it is too personal or if they just want to keep it private. Those who do want to share openly with the group do so with joy and excitement about the process. Their proclamations often encourage others to also share.

More often than not, we have needed more time than I had scheduled for this part of the process. Yet, with just a little sharing, participants themselves validate creativity as a mode of knowing, and the phenomenon of transformation is manifested for everyone to see. It is demystified and appears as a normal and *accessible* function of soul.

To encourage nonjudgmental communication at this point, I sit quietly and let participants guide the conversation along lines they choose. I withhold opinions but answer questions whenever asked. Most of the time, people are eager to read their poems, have interesting comments about their experiences throughout the whole process, and offer useful feedback about ways to alter the process. I can count on people to always share insight and growth, because they have reached a new awareness of their abilities to shape the world and understand the transformative power of soul in new ways.

Variations on a Theme

Variations in this process are interesting to experiment with and have convinced me that the activity is extremely versatile without losing its transformative potential. For instance, weather permitting, the activity is especially potent for connecting to Mother Earth if participants can be taken out of doors and directed through the steps while sitting on the ground. Most recently, I inserted a step between 6 and 7 when I asked students to pair off, hold both hands while gazing into each other's eyes, and simply look for the greatness in the other person. This variation elicited a stronger awareness of community and self. I have also asked participants to write letters (to their mother, friend, husband, significant other, or whomever they select) instead of a journal write or a poem. Rather than creating a poem, participants are sometimes directed to draw a picture or write a song.

I prefer to end with a creative act, because I believe creativity increases with practice and is directly connected to imagination. The imagination can lead us to break barriers, develop new consciousness, and experience the highest intuitive knowing. In this state, we can then experience the unity of inner and outer, seeing that all is interconnected. This activity can also become a delightful way of writing various poetic forms if those are introduced prior to the activity.

Note

1. A version of this chapter appears as an essay in J. P. Miller et al. (2005), *Holistic Learning and Spirituality in Education.*

References

Bachelard, G. (1969). *The poetics of space.* Boston: Beacon.

Kessler, R. (2000). *The soul of education.* Alexandria, VA: Association for Supervision and Curriculum Development.

Miller, J. P. (1996). *The holistic curriculum.* Toronto: Ontario Institute for Studies in Education Press.

Miller, J. P., et al. (Eds.). (2005). *Holistic learning and spirituality in education.* Albany, NY: State University of New York Press.

Palmer, P. J. (1998). *The courage to teach: Exploring the inner landscape of a teacher's life.* San Francisco: Jossey-Bass.

CHAPTER SIX

Walking in the Spirit of the Medicine Wheel

Learning to See What We Normally Do Not See

- *Overview:* This activity contains five parts: drawing the medicine wheel, reflective writing, activating volition for promises of future action, discover connections with others, and serving others. Participants learn about the gifts of the four directions and move around a medicine wheel that they create.
- *Materials:* Drawing paper, heavy cardboard such as poster board, wood slabs, or animal hide large enough for drawing the medicine wheel. I suggest starting with paper or poster board. Pencils, crayons, markers, or paint. Something to use for creating a large circle. I've used pie tins, dinner plates, and the rim of a round wastebasket. A ruler or yardstick or anything that can be used to draw straight lines across the entire circle. If circles within the outer circle are desired, a compass is useful.
- *Suggested time:* Two hours and ten minutes minimum. The times listed below are suggested times only, not requirements. This activity contains five detailed steps that could easily be extended over five separate sessions or more. If more extensive reflection or writing is desired, time may be extended. The medicine wheel may also be repeatedly used for infinite learning experiences and for creating many plans for promises of future action.
- *Types of learning:* Drawing, reflecting, analysis, writing, and discussion. This activity moves beyond a strictly cognitive approach to learning and relies on the physical, the emotional, the mental, and the spiritual ways we learn.

- *Participants:* Small groups preferred. If doing this alone, skip part 4 or modify it to attain feedback from people who have not completed the activity.
- *Rhetorical forms:* Self-selected by participant. The activity asks for writing at various spots. This writing could take the form of lists, sentences, songs, poems, essays, letters, and journal entries.
- *Prerequisite:* None

The medicine wheel is a Native American symbol that has been made available to all human beings as a journey of life that promotes the development of our hidden potentialities. It is a circle divided into four equal sections that symbolize the four directions: north, east, south, and west. The center, where all four directions are connected, symbolizes a person's volition, or will.

The lines in the medicine wheel are usually painted in four colors: white, black, yellow, and red, which represent the four races of people on the earth. Again, at the center of the wheel, all are connected. The sections of the medicine wheel may also be seen as symbolic of the four dimensions of people: mental, spiritual, emotional, and physical. These are connected and developed through the use of our volition.

The four directions can also lead us to see the interconnections between mineral, plant, animal, and human kingdoms in the universe (Bopp et al., 1984, pp. 29–32). When moving around the medicine wheel, we follow the natural rhythm of the earth, beginning in the east.

The medicine wheel, as a path for life, is a journey that promises continuous growth throughout our lives. It is also based upon wholeness and interconnections between all things. It has a deeply spiritual quality to it, and it is also very practical and easy to integrate into daily living. On a spiritual level, the medicine wheel helps us see what we do not normally see. As we move from one direction to another and interconnections are revealed, we can learn about things in ourselves and in others. We can learn about the interconnectedness of all in the world. We can learn about our past, our present, and our future.

Gifts from the Four Directions

- *East:* The east is the place of new beginnings. Think of the sun that rises each morning. It brings light. It starts life afresh. Its light is gentle, guileless, and innocent. There is spontaneity, joy, and a sense of renewal at each dawn. It is easy to feel purity and hope. In the east we

are able to love in a way that doesn't question others and doesn't call attention to itself. We have courage, truthfulness, and leadership as we guide others. We can experience beautiful speech even as we are vulnerable. We have the ability to see clearly and can focus, trusting in our own vision. We can stay tuned to the present time and concentrate with ease. The east helps us see things in perspective and lets us be devoted in our service to others. It is a place of birth and rebirth, and it illuminates us with light (Bopp et al., 1984, p. 72).
- *South:* The south is a place of fullness and summer light. It is kind, generous, and full of love. It is a place of strong growth where the senses are developed and where we are passionately involved with the world. We yearn to be with the one person we love. There is a youthful quality, and the heart is bursting with compassion as it is attracted to good and repulsed by bad, especially senseless violence. It is also a place where we find the ability to express our hurt and bad feelings as well as our joy and good feelings. We are able to set aside our strong feelings as we strive to serve others. We are able to appreciate and to express ourselves through music. It is a place of balance and development of the physical body even as our appetites are controlled. We set goals in the south and hold on to idealism (Bopp et al., 1984, p. 72).
- *West:* We go inward for meditation, dreams, and deep inner thoughts when we enter the west. Although there is darkness, it is a darkness that lends itself to intuitive knowing and reflective thoughts. We test our will in the west as we struggle to assist other people and as we reach for inner vision of our potentialities and possibilities. Humility attaches itself to us and promotes our ability to make sacrifices. These lead us to a greater awareness of our spiritual qualities. We also develop respect for our elders, for others' beliefs, and for their attempts to find spirituality. We enjoy silence, using it to promote the gifts and lessons of the west, and we learn to enjoy being alone. We develop perseverance and determination to finish tasks. Ceremony, ritual, and spiritual practices such as fasting become attractive. We learn how to recognize and manage our personal power, which often leads to spiritual insight, clear self-knowledge, and a high moral code (Bopp et al., 1984, p. 73).
- *North:* The north is a place of wisdom and maturity where tasks are completed and where we learn to live in moderation and with justice. We honor our elders, particularly for their wisdom and intellectual gifts such as thinking, analyzing, calculating and speculating, organizing, understanding, and interpreting and for their ability to see how all things

fit together. We learn how to problem solve, how to criticize, and how to discriminate in helpful ways. It is the place where we develop these same abilities that our elders demonstrate. We can develop detachment and find freedom from fear, hate, love, and even knowledge. It is also where our intuition is made conscious and we sense how to live a balanced life. We gain confidence and an ability to make predictions and to live at the center of things (Bopp et al., 1984, p. 73).

The Activity

The five parts below are designed to address a *generalized focus* on self and elements connected to the individual writer. However, this focus can be shifted to a *specific focus* on an idea, issue, or problem. To make such a shift, simply focus on the idea, issue, or problem in your mind as you complete the various steps. Let all you do pertain to that idea, issue, or problem. By doing this, the activities can be repeated all through the years of your life as a way to illuminate and discover what you have not yet seen.

Part 1: Drawing the Medicine Wheel (thirty minutes)
1. Draw a rather large circle on the surface of your drawing material.
2. Draw two straight lines across the circle so that they dissect in the center.
3. If you want to depict the center where volition is found, you can draw a smaller circle or square around the center point so that there is a circle within a circle or a square within the circle.
4. On a separate piece of paper, select gifts that appeal to you at the present time from each of the four directions.
5. For each gift, write a sentence or two that explains your choice.
6. Next, at the end of each written explanation, draw a symbol that can depict that gift. For example, you might want to use a star to symbolize confidence or an arrow to depict freedom from fear. Maybe a scale would symbolize justice or a balanced life. Select symbols that feel right for you. Numbers might appeal to you, too. Seven becomes love, nine is justice, and so forth.
7. Pick a segment for each direction on the medicine wheel. Draw your symbols and place them in strategic spots. Let your intuition guide your placement. Don't think about it very hard or even at all. Just put them where you think they look good. Use color to enhance your choices and to emphasize the symbolic meaning.

Part 2: Reflective Writing (thirty minutes)
1. Review the visual qualities of your entire medicine wheel, and write a description of them. Explain what the symbols represent, and give reasons for selecting that symbol. Begin in the east, move to the south, then the west, and finally to the north.
2. After writing about all four directions, draw conclusions about your current position in the world and how you are relating to the people, events, and places in your life at this time.
3. Draw conclusions about your soul, the society of which you are a part, and about your relationship to the earth.
4. Try to identify the items that are motivating you the strongest. Include a statement about where you would next like to go or in what area you would like your development to be focused.

Part 3: Activating Volition for Promises of Future Action (thirty minutes)

Volition is the energy we use to motivate ourselves, whether that is making decisions or taking actions. It is placed at the center of the wheel because it connects the gifts from the four directions and is the primary force to use to develop these gifts. Volition can be exercised by activating five steps:

1. attention (concentration)
2. goal setting
3. initiating the action
4. perseverance
5. completing the action (Bopp et al., 1984, p. 14)

If there are more gifts, at this time, appearing in the east, it might be a time for you to make specific decisions or to take specific actions to further develop those gifts.

1. Look at what you have already written, select a single item on which you would like to focus, and write a plan of action to develop it. From which direction does this item come? Decide if you can use other gifts in that same direction to support this item. Also look at the other three directions to select gifts that complement your development of this item.
2. From the five steps above, select the appropriate ones to use as you plan to develop this item.

3. Write a plan of action for developing your growth with this item.
4. Write down what you expect to gain from developing this item.
5. To conclude, write about how this plan stimulates your soul, your place in society, and your relationship with the earth.

Part 4: Discover Connections with Others (thirty minutes)
1. Pick two or three people to spend time with.
2. Display your medicine wheel to the group, and read aloud your writing.
3. As you listen to others, write a list of items that are the same as yours.
4. When everyone has shared, before group discussion write a list of things you now see about your own plan that you didn't see before.
5. Finally, discuss the plans for future growth, and offer comments or suggestions for modifications. Record those that seem appealing for your use.

Part 5: Serving Others (ten minutes)
To conclude, write about how your plan serves your soul, your society, and the earth. Decide where your plan mostly serves, and imagine how it might be extended to serve more broadly.

Reference

Bopp, J., Bopp, M., Brown, L., & Lane, P. (1984). *The sacred tree*. Alberta, Canada: Four Worlds Development Press.

CHAPTER SEVEN

Mapping Art and Beauty to Solve Problems

- *Overview*: Participants will receive and activate a visual mapping process of change derived from theories of creativity and beauty. They will contemplate a problem, play with art and beauty as a process to discover the solution, and learn to value art as a necessity in life as well as a practical approach to problem solving.
- *Materials*: Pen or pencil, colored pencils, mapping with art page (see figure 7.1)
- *Optional materials*: Additional drafting paper and/or other art supplies as desired
- *Suggested time*: Twenty to forty-five minutes
- *Types of learning*: Verbal, visual, reflective, analytic, emotional, physical, spiritual, and social
- *Participants*: Participants work alone to solve a problem they select and then choose to share or not share with other participants.
- *Rhetorical forms*: Creative writing, problem solving, and reflective analysis
- *Prerequisite*: Participants need a situation or problem that they want to address with creative problem solving.

The Activity

Step 1: At the root of *imagine* is *image*. According to the research completed on imagery and creativity by George Ainsworth-Land, the relationship between creativity and imagery is developmental. People can identify and use a creative process:

The first impulse is sense related and arises out of physical need.

1. Pick one problem in your life that needs a solution.
2. List emotions that you associate with that problem.
3. Surround your thoughts with these words from Roger Scruton's book *Beauty: A Very Short Introduction* (2011) on the theory of beauty: "Contemplation fills us with wonder, and prompts us to search for meaning and value in the cosmos" (p. 55).

Step 2: The second step involves improvement of an idea or artistic product through analysis and evaluation.

1. Analyze the context of the problem.
2. List the parts that are within your control.
3. List the parts that are controlled by others.
4. List the parts that are flexible and welcome modification.
5. List the parts that are intractable or impossible to change.
6. On a scale of one to ten (one is the lowest amount of difficulty), rank the level of effort or difficulty that is caused by the controlling features.
7. Reflect on these words from Scruton, and imagine beauty being a balm that removes difficulty: "Art . . . takes us out of our everyday practical concerns, by providing us with objects, characters, scenes and actions with which we can play, and which we can enjoy for what they are, rather than for what they do for us. . . . In play, elevated by art to the level of free contemplation, reasons and sense are reconciled, and we are granted a vision of human life in its wholeness" (p. 107).

Step 3: The third requires synthesis, not just revision or modification. Something new or novel must be discovered through the synthesis before there is a breakthrough to new knowledge or understanding.

1. Create an artistic representation (poem, song, drawing, story, or other) of the context that surrounds the problem. Let the act of creativity lead you to a solution.
2. Contemplate what Scruton has to say: "True artists control their subject-matter, in order that our response to it should be *their* doing, not *ours*" (p. 90).

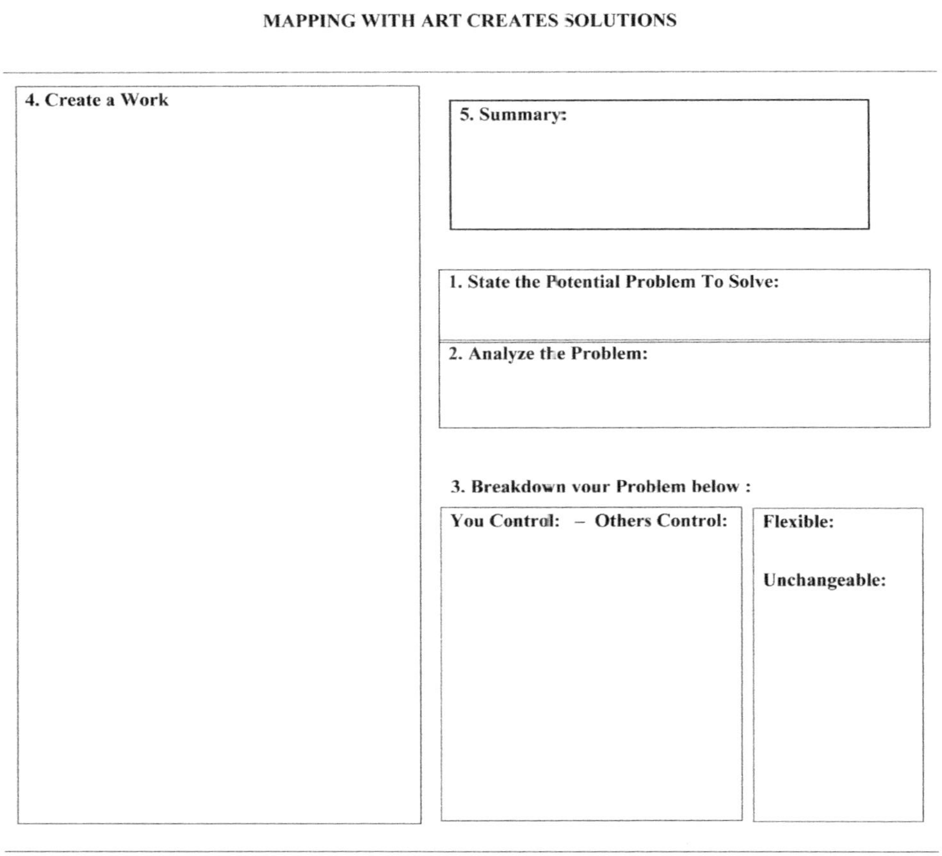

MAPPING WITH ART CREATES SOLUTIONS

5. Summary:

1. State the Potential Problem To Solve:

2. Analyze the Problem:

3. Breakdown your Problem below :

You Control: – Others Control:

Flexible:

Unchangeable:

4. Create a Work

Figure 7.1.

Step 4: The final step, Ainsworth-Land states, occurs when "one's whole being comes into play with the conscious and unconscious minds, reason and intuition, inner and outer, subsumed into a kind of meta-consciousness. . . . The self is part of a larger reality. [Here, one is] building new perceptual order" (quoted in J. P. Miller, 1996, p. 94).

1. Write a brief statement that explains how artistic expression and creativity has revealed a view of the problem and solution that you were unaware of before using this process.
2. Hold Scruton's idea in mind: "Art points to *another way of being*" (p. 139).

Step 5: Conclusion: time to share

References

MacCarthy, F. (2011, March 25). The aesthetic movement. *Guardian* (UK ed.), p. 16.

Miller, J. P. (1996). *The holistic curriculum*. Toronto: Ontario Institute for Studies in Education Press.

Scruton, R. (2011). *Beauty: A very short introduction*. Oxford: Oxford University Press.

Note

The mapping with art creates a solutions page that was designed by Rebecca Zeiss. A color graphic is available at : http://zeissworks.com/images/map.jpg.

CHAPTER EIGHT

Write Your Own Ending

- *Overview*: Participants read part of a play and then write their own ending for it. A group discussion featuring the new endings and comparing them to the original ending follows the writing. During the discussion, relevant topics from the play's content are explored.
- *Materials*: Pen and paper
- *Suggested time*: One hour, minimum. This can easily be stretched out depending on variations writers or facilitators initiate.
- *Types of learning*: Connecting art, history, social science, drama, and philosophy. Physical, emotional, mental, social, environmental, and spiritual. This activity can be used as a smaller part of a larger unit on drama or used alone.[1]
- *Participants*: Small groups preferred
- *Rhetorical forms*: Drama
- *Prerequisite*: Partial play reading
- *Facilitator preparation*: Play selection. For the sake of providing a specific context, the one-act, one-set play, K2, by Patrick Meyers, (2003) has been selected. Another short story, novel, or play could be selected. K2 is an extended argument between two friends who are mountain climbing. Caught in an avalanche at twenty-seven thousand feet, one man is injured, unable to descend or ascend. He argues for his friend to leave him, knowing he will die. Does his friend leave or stay? If the friend stays, he too shall die. K2 presents a situation in nature that demands an intense ethical decision regarding life and death. It raises

philosophical questions about faith, the role of friendship, duty to family, self-development choices, and responses to tragedy. It also demands that readers examine their attitudes toward nature, natural calamity, and the human role in nature. The facilitator should read the literary selection first and decide how much writers should read before writing their own ending.

The Activity

1. Writers should receive copies of the partial play and read it before completing the steps below.
2. In groups of two to four, writers can discuss how they would end the play.
3. Groups write their own ending.
4. After all the groups have written their ending, each group presents it to the others and gives reasons for their choices.
5. A general discussion regarding choices can guide the groups.
6. Groups are given the original ending to read.
7. A closing discussion on the play's original ending, on the differences presented by the various groups' endings, and on rhetorical choices writers make when writing drama concludes the activity.

Note

1. "Write Your Own Ending" was originally created by Clint Burhans to fulfill a requirement in English 460, Senior Seminar: Issues in English, at Central Michigan University (CMU). In his project, this activity was presented as a small segment within a large multidisciplinary, semester-long course aimed at adolescents attending Windsor House Alternative School in Vancouver, British Columbia. Students at this school are free to study what they wish when they wish. Burhans' course used drama to unite the various disciplines he wanted to blend into a holistic learning experience. He asked students to write, produce, and perform their own play. *K2* and the Write Your Own Ending activity was an introduction to dramatic form, audience expectations, and how content can determine a writer's choices. He stated that he wanted students "to learn how drama is used to express thoughts and feelings about the world, and how they can find out about their own thoughts and feelings through the words and actions of others." When Burhans facilitated this activity in the senior capstone presentation (a graduation requirement at CMU), the participants responded well to it and enjoyed a lively conversation about the ethical and environmental issues presented in *K2*. It was a highly successful presentation and was

selected for use in this book on those grounds. Burhans was kind enough to grant permission for its use here.

References

Meyers, P. (2003). K2. In J. Standord (Ed.), *Responding to literature: Stories, poems, plays and essays* (pp. 891–913, 4th ed.) Boston: McGraw Hill.

CHAPTER NINE

The Connected Self

- *Overview*: Participants write a self-profile, a partner profile, or a combination of these after exploring holistic qualities (emotional, physical, intellectual, social, aesthetic(beauty), spiritual, and universal) of their partners and themselves. The writing process of drafting, writing, and revising is suggested. Writers also need to select an audience for their writing and specific rhetorical strategies to use when writing.
- *Materials*: Freezer paper or drawing paper; crayons, markers, colored pencils, and any other art supplies desired; writing paper and pen

Suggested time: Time can be determined by the writers or the facilitator. Time is needed for four parts:

1. Prewriting activities
2. The writing process
3. Reflective meta-writing
4. Celebrating the connected self

- *Types of learning*: Verbal, visual, mental, emotional, physical, spiritual, and social
- *Participants*: Partners
- *Rhetorical forms*: Biographical and autobiographical essay
- *Prerequisite*: None

The Activity

Part 1: Prewriting Activities
1. Each participant should fill out the form titled "Holistic Self-Profile." Let intuition guide your response. Do not "think" about your response at all; just write down the first words that come to your mind.
2. Each participant should then draw a circle on the drawing paper provided; then in the circle, draw an abstract image for each metaphor you wrote on this form.
3. Partnerships need to be formed next.
4. Partners should discuss each other's drawings, including any insights, surprises, or expectations they may have discovered in this process. On a separate piece of paper, jot down a few notes about these for use when you draft the essay.
5. Identify qualities you shared with each other during this process. Again, jot these down on a separate piece of paper.
6. Partners should fill out the form titled "Shared Qualities."
7. Partners then draw an oblong oval that can serve as a bridge or connector for each of their individual circles. Then draw abstract symbols for the metaphors written on this form. Partners should end up with a visual that contains their two circles that are connected by the oblong bridge.

Part 2: The Writing Process
1. Participants need to decide whether they want to write alone or work collaboratively. If they decide to collaborate, they produce one essay only. If they decide to work alone, they still seek support and guidance from their partner during the writing process.
2. Writers select an audience for their essay and decide what information this audience finds most useful and why they might want to obtain it.
3. Writers select a rhetorical aim (persuasive, informative, or expressive; see appendix B).
4. Partners select an appropriate organizational strategy to use when writing the essay. They might choose from classification, compare, contrast, narration, description, definition, process analysis or casual analysis, and illustration (see appendix B). Using a combination of strategies is also an option. Writers should feel free to shift strategies as needed when writing the essay.

Title the essay "The Connected Self," and select a focus. Focus selection is somewhat directed by audience and aim. You may want to focus on

- self-profile (autobiography),
- partner profile (biography), or
- both (combining the above).

5. Write the first draft.
6. Review the first draft with your partner.
7. Make revision decisions.
8. Write the second draft.
9. Repeat the review and revision process as many times as you think necessary.
10. Reach a final draft.

Part 3: Reflective Meta-writing

Attach a closing statement that lists the following elements in the final draft:

1. Audience
2. Aim
3. Focus
4. Strengths
5. What was omitted or changed from previous drafts
6. What the writers like about their essay
7. What the writers don't like about their essay
8. A comment about prewriting activities that explains to what degree the activities were helpful.

Part 4: Celebrating the Connected Self

For Classroom Formats

The teacher or facilitator can initiate a group discussion that invites writers to

1. share what they learned about themselves;
2. share what they learned about their partner;
3. discuss the prewriting activities;
4. discuss the writing process;
5. discuss their emotions about any of the above;

6. suggest ways of improving the activities;
7. suggest ways the prewriting activities might be used to generate other written genres such as poetry or song lyrics; and
8. give reasons they may or may not feel more connected to themselves or others in the class.

For Individual Writers

Writers might want to write a follow-up essay that features ideas suggested for writers in a classroom format. Or they may want to have a conversation about their experiences with someone who is uninformed about the activities—perhaps a friend, parent, grandparent, sibling, or neighbor.

Holistic Self-Profile

Instructions
1. Fill in the blanks with single words or short phrases.
2. Don't take time to think about the words; just use the first word that comes to mind. Let your intuition guide you.
3. After filling out the chart, represent each word written with a symbolic image on drawing paper.

Shared Qualities

Instructions
1. Fill in the blanks with single words or short phrases that are the same or are similar to those that appear on both Holistic Self-Profiles.
2. Discuss the similarities *and* discuss those that were not included on the shared qualities form.

Holistic Self-Profile

Aspects	Static (No change)	Dynamic (Changes)	Metaphoric (Symbolic Comparison)
Emotional			
Physical			
Intellectual			
Social			
Beauty			
Spiritual			
Universal			

Shared Qualities

Aspects	Static (No change)	Dynamic (Changes)	Metaphoric (Symbolic Comparison)
Emotional			
Physical			
Intellectual			
Social			
Beauty			
Spiritual			
Universal			

CHAPTER TEN

Visioning in Silent Community

- *Overview*: Participants read a short literary selection (I have used selections from fiction, nonfiction prose, and poetry).[1] Each participant selects two or three key quotes that may represent the overall meaning in the literature. Then, with a partner and in silence, participants draw a nonrepresentational (abstract) image of meaning that corresponds to one selected passage. During this process, participants shall not write notes or use verbal language to communicate with their partner. After the drawing is completed, participants write a brief explanation of the image. The final stage is to form a "community collage" and discuss it as well as the process used to create it. The collage is a visual and tangible element; it melds the phenomenological variance that naturally and spiritual arises out of the silent space people use for creativity and literary visioning in silent community.
- *Materials*: Markers, crayons, color pencils, poster board, writing paper, pens or pencils, scotch tape, and scissors
- *Suggested time*: Sixty to ninety minutes
- *Types of learning*: Reading, drawing, writing, reflecting, and discussing; physical, emotional, mental, verbal, visual, spatial, and spiritual
- *Participants*: Partners and whole class sizes, such as twenty-five to thirty people
- *Rhetorical forms*: Paragraphs or short essay
- *Prerequisite*: Advanced reading ability

Preliminary preparation for facilitator:

1. On the reverse side of each poster board, draw a line that divides the poster board into two jigsaw puzzle shapes. Each part of the first poster board is numbered "1," so you will have two 1s, two 2s, two 3s, and so forth. Then cut the poster board into puzzle parts. You should end up with a collection of jigsaw pieces that can easily be reassembled later by simply looking for both 1s, 2s, 3s, and so on.
2. Select a short reading passage that can be read in about five minutes, and make enough copies of it for all participants to use. Nonfiction, fiction, and poetry work well for this activity.
3. At the beginning it is useful to emphasize that the silence in the activity facilitates the spiritual and practical use of silence and art as a means to interpret literary texts and to build classroom community. A preliminary statement to this effect invites the silence and contextualizes it to a point that people desire to cooperate. Silence is quite uncomfortable and difficult for some people to use. The context helps give those people a reason to persevere and to tolerate their discomfort if it should arise. It is also helpful to give people "permission" to silently leave the room if the silence is just too hard to accommodate.
4. Make enough copies of the instructions for each partnership to refer to during the time of silence. This helps if they should have questions.

The Activity

1. The facilitator passes out copies of the literature and copies of the instructions.
2. This activity uses a lot of silence. Please hold all questions until the silence is broken at the end of the activity.
3. Pick a partner.
4. Select one passage or idea from the reading that seems important to both of you. Please, do not talk. You may point to parts in the reading selection that you might want to consider.
5. After selecting the passage or idea, write it (exactly as it appears in the text) on the side of the poster board that is already numbered, and then write this passage on a separate piece of paper. This is used in a later step.

6. On the side of the poster board that is not numbered, create a colorful abstract image that reflects the meaning in the passage or idea you have selected. Please, do not write notes or use verbal language to communicate with your partner. Try to use the entire surface of the poster board.
7. When you are finished drawing, write a brief explanation of your image on the piece of paper from step 5. The facilitator collects these at the end of our discussion.
8. Give the drawing to the facilitator who then builds a collage as people finish writing.
9. Finally, each participant should write a brief personal response to (a) silence, (b) their drawing, and (c) the group collage. The facilitator collects these after the discussion.
10. When you are finished writing, please put your pen down. After everyone is finished writing, we break silence and discuss our experiences.
11. If you are finished before other people, please do not break silence until the facilitator gives a signal.
12. General whole group discussion.

Note

1. This activity was presented at the International Holistic Education Conference: Breaking New Ground, Toronto, 2003. It was presented again in 2013 at the 20th annual International Conference on Holistic Education in Guadalajara, Mexico.

CHAPTER ELEVEN

Screenplay Writing

- *Overview:* Participants write a partial screenplay based on a short story. This provides opportunities for literary and cinematic analysis, particularly of literary elements and cinematic elements that are needed during creative writing and during the adaptation process.
- *Materials:* A collection of short stories; samples of professional screenplays; and word-processing software and computers
- *Optional materials:* Drawing paper and markers for creating story boards; recording equipment for burning CDs or creating tapes; and *The Elements of Writing About Literature and Film* by Elizabeth McMahan, Robert Funk, and Susan Day (1988)
- *Suggested time:* Thirty-six hours minimum
- *Types of learning:* Verbal, visual, mental, emotional, physical, spiritual, and social
- *Participants:* Writers might work alone, with a partner, or in groups of three or four. Groups larger than four generally have difficulty arranging writing time that suits all members.
- *Rhetorical forms:* Creative writing, literary analysis, reflective evaluations, and informative prose
- *Prerequisite:* Writers need to have completed reading a collection of short stories before beginning this activity. Writers need to be familiar with literary elements and cinematic elements. See the lists at the end of this chapter, and see McMahan, Funk, and Day (1988) for definitions or descriptions. Writers need to have discussed the factors that

create the unique circumstances that govern literary writing and those that govern filmmaking (in other words, why a book cannot be exactly like a film and a film cannot be exactly like a book).

The Activity

1. After reading a collection of short stories, select a single story *or* a sequence of scenes from one story upon which to base your screenplay.
2. Decide how far you wish to "depart" from the original plot.

The final project should include in this order:

a. A cover sheet with title and name(s)
b. A brief analysis of the whole collection of short stories that describes strengths and weaknesses. This page documents that the whole book has been read and understood.
c. A list of literary elements used in the screenplay
d. A list of cinematic elements used in the screenplay
e. A casting list that names actors and actresses and describes a type of actor and actress
f. A list of music selections (optional: A CD or tape containing the music selections in the order as they appear in the screenplay. If one selection is used three times, it would also appear three times on the CD or tape.)
g. The screenplay in screenplay format[1]
h. A list of "departures" made from the story and the reasons they were made
i. A self-evaluation of the work. If working in groups, there should be one evaluation for each group member, written by that person.
j. A group evaluation about ways the group worked together (if applicable). There should be one evaluation written by the group.

Literary Elements
- Allusion
- Ambiguity
- Antagonist
- Catharsis
- Character development
- Chronological order
- Classical dramatic structure

- Coherence
- Dialogue
- Dramatic irony
- Epiphany
- Flashbacks
- Foil
- Foreshadowing
- Hyperbole
- Metaphor
- Mood
- Motif
- Plot
- Point of view (there are four major types: omniscient, dramatic, limited, and unreliable)
- Protagonist
- Setting
- Simile
- Stereotype
- Subplot
- Symbolism
- Theme

Cinematic Elements
In addition to the literary elements above, film can contain the following:

- Casting
- Close-ups
- Color
- Crosscutting
- Cutaway
- Cut-in
- Cuts
- Dissolves
- Extreme close-ups
- Fade-ins
- Fade-outs
- Film and slides
- Full shots
- Keys
- Lighting

- Long shots
- Medium close-ups
- Medium shots
- Music and/or sound
- Over-the-shoulder shots
- Props
- Reaction short
- Sequence
- Slit screens
- Superimpositions
- Surveying pan
- Two shot, three shot
- Wipes
- Zoom in
- Zoom out

Note

1. Screenplay format varies in form. I tell writers to create a consistent format of their own, that is, all subheadings might be bold, dialogue, centered, and so forth.

Reference

McMahan, E., Funk R., & Day, S. (1988). *The elements of writing about literature and film.* New York: Macmillan.

CHAPTER TWELVE

Info-Commercial

- *Overview:* The info-commercial is a fifteen-minute mini-drama, based on the classical dramatic structure (exposition, rising action, climax, falling action, and denouement), that persuades the audience to read, or not to read, a particular novel, short story, poem, play, or essay. Participants are asked to include interconnections to soil, soul, and society.
- *Materials:* Pen and paper; large sheets of construction paper; and "Response Guides." Props are to be determined by the participants.
- *Suggested time:* To be determined by number of participants. Time for outside planning is needed as is time for presenting the info-commercial. Time for reviewing "Response Guides" and for reflecting on ways to improve the info-commercial. Time for drafting a short essay that describes future improvements to the info-commercial.
- *Participants:* Small groups are preferred, but partners or individuals could complete this activity.
- *Types of learning:* Visual, verbal (written and spoken), physical, intellectual, emotional, spiritual, social, environmental, and reflective
- *Rhetorical forms:* Persuasive drama and reflective, analytic prose
- *Prerequisite:* Participants might select their own book or essay to base their info-commercial on or the facilitator could provide one. Each group should have a different title, so the facilitator needs to check on this if participant selection occurs.

- *Precautions:* Prohibit violence or extreme sexual situations. Participants should be encouraged to use a style or approach that is safe, fun, and respectful rather than those that might be considered as X-rated or as sensationalized negativity.

The Activity

Part 1
1. Form small groups.
2. Each group should select a novel, play, short story, poem, or essay to use for this activity and read it.

Part 2
1. List all the literary reasons that might convince someone to read this piece of literature. For example, maybe the writing style flows easily and is accessible, or perhaps the ideas are relevant to the audience members.
2. List all the literary reasons that might prevent someone from reading this piece of literature. For example, maybe the writing style is too wordy, or the ideas are too philosophical.
3. Review each list and select a focus for the info-commercial. Does it persuade people to read the piece of literature, or does it persuade them not to read it?
4. Chart the plot. At the top of a large piece of construction paper, draw a line and label the parts of the classical dramatic structure on the appropriate spots.
5. Below each section, list the key points of action that are contained in each section. For example, all the background information needed for creating the context is listed under exposition; action that builds to the turning point is listed under rising action; under climax, the turning point is described; actions that follow the climax are listed under falling action; and the final closing action that wraps everything up is listed under denouement.

Part 3
1. Select roles to perform in the info-commercial.
2. Write a script for the info-commercial.
3. Make a list of props to be used, and decide how and from where to obtain these. Props might include a special wardrobe.

Part 4
Rehearse the info-commercial.

Part 5
Perform the info-commercial.

Part 6
1. Audience members can use the "Response Guide" to record their immediate impressions as they are watching the info-commercials being performed.
2. Each group receives all the "Response Guides" after their performance is completed.

Part 7
1. After all the info-commercials have been performed, each group reviews the "Response Guides" to reflect on their creative work.
2. Each group collaboratively drafts a short essay that explains how the info-commercial might be changed to become even more persuasive and to review connections to soil, soul, and society.

Response Guide

Literature title _____

1. The group wants people to read this literature.   Yes   No
2. List reasons that you heard given for the above recommendation.
3. I will read this piece of literature because . . .
4. I will not read this piece of literature because . . .
5. What part of the classical dramatic structure was most effective in this info-commercial: exposition, rising action, climax, falling action, or denouement?
6. Soil, soul, and society were appropriately interconnected. No Partially yes
7. Add other comments that help the group strengthen their info-commercial.

CHAPTER THIRTEEN

Cave Art

Is It Literature? Is It Writing?

- *Overview:* This four-part activity involves film viewing, drawing, discussing, researching, and writing about cave art. Participants decide if cave art is literature, writing, or both. History, environmental pressures on ancient human and animal populations, and the relationship of art to early childhood language acquisition are embedded in the activities.[1]
- *Materials:* Brown paper lunch bags or grocery bags, markers or crayons, tape, movie *Ice Age*, wall space, TV or VCR, and paper and pen
- *Suggested time:* Part 1, one hour; part 2, one hour; part 3, three to ten hours; part 4, five to ten hours
- *Participants:* Individuals, partners, or small groups
- *Types of learning:* Visual, verbal (written and spoken), physical, intellectual, emotional, spiritual, social, environmental, and reflective
- *Rhetorical forms:* Fiction, autobiography, and report writing
- *Prerequisite:* Access to a local library and or Internet search engines; and knowledge of source documentation style, such as APA, MLA, or others
- *Precautions:* The facilitator might want to present an overview of the entire activity for the purpose of selecting (with the participants) time guidelines on each part.

The Activity

Part 1
For individuals (one hour)

1. Watch scene twelve from the movie *Ice Age*.[2]
2. Discuss the movie clip—what was the cave art showing or saying?
3. Introduce and read a short story, for example, a fable or parable.
4. Pass out paper bags.
5. Instruct participants to crumple up their bags to give a cave look to their paper and then to smooth it back out flat.
6. Instruct participants now to draw their own cave art that depicts a fictional story or a story of their own lives.
7. As the art is completed, tape it to the wall space.
8. When all the cave art is on the wall, have each participant explain his or her story.

Part 2
Partner or small-group collaboration (one hour)

After the whole group discussion above, instruct participants to write a description of the cave art for an audience that has not yet seen it or might never see it. The description should reveal physical, social, mental, aesthetic, emotional, and spiritual aspects that they see. The overall purpose of cave art and the activity to this point can also be included.

Part 3
Partner or small-group collaboration in research (time as needed in a library or on the Internet; three to ten hours suggested)

1. Instruct participants to find facts about cave art in various parts of the world that they can use to compare and contrast with their own group cave art wall. These facts may also feature information about extinct species or human conditions.
2. Instruct participants to find facts about the role of art in early childhood (ages 2–7) language acquisition and development.
3. Ask participants to take a position on whether cave art is literature, writing, or perhaps both.

Part 4
Partner or small-group synthesis and collaboration in report writing (time is to be determined by the group; five to ten hours suggested)

Instruct participants to collaborate as they write a report that interconnects their research with the cave art drawing and writing experience from parts 1 and 2. Each partnership or small group produces one essay.

Part 5: Closure
Conduct a group discussion about the writing and discoveries that arose out of the writing.

Notes

1. Samantha Clark and Tessa Holman (Central Michigan University students in English 460, Senior Seminar: Current Issues in English) designed part 1 for use in first grade at the Austin Waldorf School. Parts 2, 3, and 4 make the activity suitable for an older and more experienced participant. Clark and Holman's presentation of part 1 during class presentations (fall semester 2004) went exceedingly well. After viewing the movie clip, an animated text, students stretched out on the floor or moved around to find a comfortable spot to draw their cave art. During the group discussion, we learned more about each other, since most of the art was autobiographical, and ideas about extinct species and human cultural practices either lost or dropped expanded the discussion beyond English. The discussion became interdisciplinary in a natural way. I believe this activity facilitated interconnections and holistic learning very successfully without being forced or self-conscious. Clark and Holman were delighted by my request to use their material and granted permission for me to do so.

2. This clip shows the characters observing cave art that depicts extinct species and family life among the species.

Reference

Donkin, J. C., Forte, L., & Meledander, C. (Producers); Wedge, C., & Saldanha, C. (Directors). (2002). *Ice Age* (Motion Picture). Los Angeles: 20th Century Fox.

CHAPTER FOURTEEN

Finding Your Community's Literature

- *Overview:* This activity broadens the understanding and place of writing in our everyday lives and in our community.[1] Participants conduct a community field study to gather found literature. They then create a group collage and analyze the motivation, purpose, and expression of "found literature" in the community.
- *Materials:* Cameras or digital cameras; computer, visualizer, or overhead projector; a big white sheet of paper and tape; pens, markers, paper, and artifact documentation cards; stapler with staples, journals, and magazines
- *Suggested time:* Sixty minutes for preparation; community time to be determined by the group or facilitator; sixty minutes for sharing and discussion of "found" literature; sixty minutes for journal writing
- *Participants:* Individuals, partners, or small groups
- *Types of learning:* Visual, verbal (written and spoken), physical, intellectual, emotional, spiritual, social, environmental, and reflective
- *Rhetorical forms:* Journal writing
- *Prerequisite:* Basic skills of reading and writing; and operation of a camera or digital camera and the computer to upload pictures
- *Precautions:* A handout identifying rules and restrictions for gathering "found literature" should be distributed prior to community exploration (see the end of this chapter).

The Activity

"Found literature" can be seen by direct observation of written artifacts throughout the community. They are generally found embedded in other forms. For example, you might find a bulletin board with announcements of local events. A passage from one might strike you as particularly "literary" or "poetic." Most often, found literature takes the shape of poetry. This makes "found poems" easier to see than other genres that require more length and detail.

When identifying a found poem, look for words that are sequenced so that meaning other than the surface or intended meaning might be seen. Usually, found literature is discovered within another piece of writing and is not the entire piece of writing it is found within. You cannot add words to the section you believe to be a "found piece of literature." So . . . this means a found piece of literature is a segment of a larger piece and is intact within the larger piece. It can be a string of words, phrases, or sentences.

Found literature can also be discovered by omitting words, phrases, or sentences within the sequence. For example, sentence 3 of the original might be sentence 1 of your found piece and the original sentence 6 might be sentence 2 of the found piece.

Discovering found literature requires seeing written artifacts in new order and with new meaning. It means looking at billboards, signs, advertisements, fliers, posters, newspaper articles, nonfiction pieces, technical reports, graffiti, and all genres of written expression with a new set of eyes.

Part 1: Preparation for Community Field Work
The facilitator should do the following:

1. Introduce and describe the purpose and directions of the activity.
2. Distribute handout and allow questions.
3. Encourage students to work with others.
4. Distribute magazines to all the students, and instruct them to look for "found literature." This is a warm-up for when they are engaged in community fieldwork.
5. Review genres of written expression participants might consider when in the field.
6. Allow time for students to make a plan of action for fieldwork. For example, they might make a list of possible places to visit and types of genres to look for or at. They might make a timetable that shows when, where, and with whom they visit that site. They might make a list of materials they need to take along on their field study.
7. Review and give instructions about gathering material in the field.

Part 2: Community Fieldwork
1. Allow the participants time for locating found literature in the community.
2. Instruct them to take photographs of the original written artifacts.

If photographs are too difficult or impossible to get, instruct participants to record their originals in a notebook for later reference. While photographs are *exact* reference points from which the setting or context of the found literature is understood, a written record of the same suffices. This information is needed when forming a synthesis about the community is undertaken in part 4.

Part 3: Forming a Collage

1. Have participants share their collected found literature. They should identify the genre and tell where it was found. They can also speculate on what motivated the literature and what emotions and meaning are evoked in the new found literature once it is seen.
2. Create a collage or bulletin board of all the collected artifacts.

Part 4: Community Synthesis
1. Have participants write a short analysis of the collage.
2. The facilitator might want the group to generate a list of issues they can consider before synthesizing the collage.
3. What does the collage say about literature? What does it say about the place of writing in our community? What does it say about the community? What does it say about the places it was found? What does it say about the people who found it? What general impression about the community can a non-community member receive from the collage?
4. What message might someone receive about soul, soil, and society after reflecting on separate parts of the collage and or on the whole collage?

Precautions and Reminders
While you are exploring your community for "found literature," keep these things in mind:

Do
1. Tell your guardian where you are going and for what reason.
2. Always get permission before leaving.
3. Do your searching during daylight hours only.

4. Go in a group of people. Have friends or family members join you on your journey.

Do Not
1. Trespass onto private property.
2. Take pieces that are in use or have been placed for a purpose (e.g., If you see a flyer posted on a bulletin board, do not rip it down; instead, take a picture of it.)
3. Cause disturbances (e.g., Do not speak loudly when searching through a library.)

Good Places
  Churches
  Community centers
  Libraries and schools
  Sidewalks
  Bulletin boards

Bad Places
  Bars
  Warehouses
  Construction sites
  Alleyways
  Dumpsters

  Smart People Make Smart Decisions

Note

1. This activity, originally titled "Your Community's Literature," was created by Joel D. Annunzio, Kelly Stevens, Emily Homrich, and Susanne Peck from English 460, Senior Seminar: Issues in English. I have used it with their permission, but I have extensively modified it. The collage they created during their class presentation stimulated a lot of interesting discussion about community values and environmental conditions that shape people and communities.

CHAPTER FIFTEEN

～

Creating a Life's Legacy

- *Overview:* This activity requires participants to set future goals by which their lives are judged at the time of their deaths.[1] They are encouraged to produce a personal connection between time, death, and epitaphs as a form of legacy. They read, interpret, and discuss famous epitaphs as a prelude to writing their own. They plan future goals that can lead to a significant legacy that is summarized or symbolized in some way by their epitaph. They then write their own epitaphs and volunteer it to be read aloud to them by others. A more extensive writing follows.
- *Materials:* Pen and paper; a mat or blanket; samples of poems and famous epitaphs (see the end of this chapter); construction paper for making epitaphs; and markers or crayons
- *Suggested time:* One to two hours for parts 1, 2, and 3, followed by sufficient writing time
- *Participants:* Individuals or small groups
- *Types of learning:* Visual, verbal (written and spoken), physical, intellectual, emotional, spiritual, social, environmental, and reflective
- *Rhetorical forms:* This activity could lead to a number of written genres, for example, songs; poems; short stories; plays that enact the goals; reflective or analytic essays; process essays of instructions to reach the goals; letters to parents, siblings, or children; and journal writing.
- *Prerequisite:* Familiarity with the scene from Mark Twain's *Adventures of Tom Sawyer* when Tom witnesses his own funeral; and familiarity with the way time influences setting and cultural attitudes.

- *Precautions:* It is imperative to stay focused on life and the quality of life, rather than on death. Individuals' ability to recognize their soul, follow its demands, contribute to their society, and sustain our earth should be featured in discussions. The epitaph, emphasized as a legacy, makes a statement about life not death, and it can awaken a new awareness of what can be manifested in life.

The Activity

Part 1: Literary Preparation
Small groups or one large group

1. Review Tom Sawyer's funeral scene from *The Adventures of Tom Sawyer* (chapter 17). Discussion needs to include issues of time and its relevance to the people and their attitudes about Tom's life. Tom's ability to self-reflect and to develop new awareness about his life can assist in creating the strong emphasis on life that is needed in this activity.
2. Define epitaph, its ability to leave a legacy, and its cultural importance.
3. Review famous epitaphs, speculate about the person's life, and identify the legacy left by the epitaph (see the end of this chapter).

Part 2: Planning the Legacy
Individuals

1. Make a plan for your life legacy. Identify achievements, goals, and personal and professional characteristics to develop. Create a time line for manifesting this plan.
2. Write an epitaph that symbolizes or summarizes your life's legacy.
3. Cut out a headstone shape from the construction paper, and write the epitaph on it. Illustrate it accordingly, if desired.

Part 3: Sharing the Legacy
Whole group and individuals

1. Read aloud the epitaphs.

Part 4: Writing About the Legacy
Individuals

1. Allow time for journal writing.
2. Allow time for an extended writing in a particular genre. All writing should include additional development of participants' plans to manifest their personal legacies.

Anonymous Epitaphs

> She skied
> But loved the sea yet loved her family more
> Thus she quietly waits in this beautiful place for those who love the mountains the snow
> Oct. 21, 1916–July 23, 1976

Playing with names in a Ruidos, New Mexico, cemetery:

> Here lies Johnny Yeast Pardon me for not rising.

A lawyer's epitaph in England:

> Sir John Strange
> Here lies an honest lawyer, And that is Strange.

On Margaret Daniel's grave at Hollywood Cemetery Richmond, Virginia:

> She always said her feet were killing her but nobody believed her.

Anna Hopewell's grave in Enosburg Falls, Vermont:

> Here lies the body of our Anna
> Done to death by a banana
> It wasn't the fruit that laid her low
> But the skin of the thing that made her go.

From the gravestone of John White, London:

> Here lies John
> A burning shining light
> Whose name, life and actions
> Were all alike

All white
Love only knoweth whence it came and comprehendith love
March 6, 1854–March 7, 1878

One by one earth's ties are broken as we see our love decay and the hopes so fondly cherished Brighten but to pass away one by one our hopes grow brighter as we near the shining shore for we know across the river wait the loved ones gone before.
April 21, 1890
53 years. 3 months 17 days

So few realize what life is about.
If I knew nothing else, I knew warmth, pleasure,
Despite everything, I knew love.
People look for what they can measure:
A degree, money, children they can brag about,
Reasons others might wish them mazel tov.
On days like other days were moments I treasured,
Life like other lives, humdrum, passing without
Yammering, with you, with the children, full enough.

Epitaphs of Famous Authors

Good Friend for Jesus Sake Forbeare To
Digg the Dust Enclosed Heare
Blest Be Ye Man Yt Spares Thes Stones and
Curst Be He Yt Moves My Bones

—William Shakespeare

Workers of All Lands Unite.
The Philosophers Have Only Interpreted the World in Various Ways; The Point is to Change it.

—Karl Marx

The body of Benjamin Franklin, printer (like the cover of an old book, its contents worn out, and stripped of its lettering and gilding) lies here, food for worms. Yet the work itself shall not lost, for it will, as he believed, appear once more in a new and more beautiful edition, corrected and amended by its Author.

—Benjamin Franklin

Against You I Will Fling Myself,
Unvanquished And Unyielding, O Death!

—Virginia Woolf

Called Back.

—Emily Dickinson

Quoth the Raven,
Nevermore.

—Edgar Allen Poe

I had a Lover's Quarrel with The World.

—Robert Frost

Nothing in Moderation,
We All Loved Him.

—Ernie Kovacs

"If [the writer] achieves anything noble, anything enduring,
it must be by giving himself absolutely to his material . . . .
He fades away into the land and people of his heart,
He dies of love only to be born again."

—Willa Cather (Powerful Words, 2013)

Note

1. This activity has been adapted from work completed by Elizabeth Shamus, Nikki Frazier, and Janae Goodchild, students in English 460, Senior Seminar: Current Issues in English (fall 2004). They believed it would fit the curriculum in place at the Community School in Camden, Maine.

References

home.wi.rr.com/epitaphs

Powerful Words. (2013). *Famous epitaphs.* Retrieved from www.famousquotes.me.uk/epitaphs.

Twain, M. (1999). *The adventures of Tom Sawyer.* New York: Children's Classics.

CHAPTER SIXTEEN

Music and Dance to Inspire the Pen

- *Overview:* This activity contains five parts that culminate in a written experience that is based on music, dance, discussion, performance, and sharing. It contains multicultural aspects that can include Internet or library research. It asks participants to fine-tune their perceptions and to understand the power of implication and inference. Participant choice is strongly featured, but the activity begins with a facilitator setting a particular tone and process for analyzing and responding to music and dance as cultural information. Depending on the music and dance selections, this activity can feature soil, soul, and society quite easily.
- *Materials:* Music and dance selections and the equipment to hear and see it; paper and pen; and space for movement
- *Suggested time:* Part 1: two to four hours; part 2: one to three hours; part 3: four to ten hours depending on time selected for music, research, and writing; part 4: ten to fifteen minutes for each performance, total time depending on whole group size; and part 5: two to six hours or as determined by participants
- *Participants:* Individuals and partners
- *Types of learning:* Visual, verbal (written and spoken), auditory, physical, intellectual, emotional, spiritual, social, environmental, and reflective
- *Rhetorical forms:* Essay; other self-selected genres possible
- *Prerequisite:* None
- *Precautions:* Participants choosing to create their own music and dance should be encouraged to avoid "cultural forms" that are based on lewd suggestions, misogyny, violence, or nudity.

The Activity

Part 1: Facilitator Preparation
The facilitator needs to do the following:

1. Select two to three examples of music or videos of dance from foreign places. These should be short enough to experience in one or two sessions.
2. Write a list of factual characteristics of the people (to be used as a handout further on).
3. List the instruments used in the music (to be used as a handout further on).
4. Identify the type of dance in the video and its cultural purpose (to be used as a handout further on).

Part 2: Participant Warm-up Writing
1. Participants listen to the music and/or see the dance video and in small groups or with a partner create a speculative profile of the people in that place that is implied by the music or dance. A list of characteristics is sufficient at this point.
2. The facilitator then passes out a list of characteristics previously compiled that is based on geographical and cultural fact. A list of instruments used in the music and/or types of dance and their purpose is also needed, since some of the sounds may be unfamiliar to the participants.
3. Participants review the "facts" and compare it with their "speculations." They need to identify specific elements in the music or dance that led to their speculations. These elements might include but are not limited to the following:

- Rhythm
- Sound
- Types of instruments
- Numbers of instruments
- Beat
- Volume
- Pitch
- Male voices
- Female voices
- Sounds from nature such as bird calls, wind, rain, or waves
- Body postures

- Dance steps
- Dance costumes
- Cadence
- Minor or major key
- Duration of music and or dance
- Blend of music and dance
- Visual sets
- Space restrictions
- Number of dancers
- Solos, duets, and so forth
- Orchestration

This writing may take the form of a list, paragraph, or short essay.

4. After the discussion, participants may write a short response that identifies what they learned about:

- Drawing inferences
- Reaching conclusions
- Perception shifts
- The importance of voice, movement, and visuals
- The atmosphere without facts
- The atmosphere with facts
- Making meaning with movement and sound
- The advantage of standing outside a culture
- The advantage of standing inside a culture

Part 3: The Personal Self and Cultural Identity

1. Individuals now select a piece of music or dance *or* create new, original music or dance that reveals something about their own personality and their own culture.

    Individuals complete two short writings:

    - A list of facts about the music or dance (see the elements listed previously). Participants can use the Internet or library to gather additional factual information at this point.
    - A short explanation of how specific elements imply or infer identity, culture, or atmosphere.

2. Participants find a partner for the next few steps and complete the following:

   - They exchange music or dance videos in order to repeat the steps in part 2.
   - They discuss their speculations afterward.

Part 4: Sharing Profiles and Culture
1. Each partnership will "show and tell" their music or dance video to the larger group and speak to specific issues they select to showcase from this activity. OR
2. Each partnership performs their original music and dance and then speaks to specific issues that they wish to showcase from their experience.

Part 5: Writing with the Inspired Pen
1. Participants can write alone or with a partner. They select the organizational strategies they wish to use in the essay.

   After part 4 has ended, participants may write an essay that identifies what they learned about the following:

   - Drawing inferences
   - Reaching conclusions
   - Perception shifts
   - The importance of voice, movement, and visuals
   - The atmosphere without facts
   - The atmosphere with facts
   - Making meaning with movement and sound
   - The advantage of standing outside a culture
   - The advantage of standing inside a culture
   - The pressure and challenge of performance
   - The joy of performing
   - Similarities between writing, dance, and music

   OR

2. They may select an alternate rhetorical genre that suits their goal as they express their whole experience with writing, dance, and music.

CHAPTER SEVENTEEN

The Writer's Scrapbook

- *Overview:* In this activity, participants read a collection of nonfiction essays and create a scrapbook of collages that presents specific ideas and images from each essay.[1] Each collage represents a different essay and depicts what the readers envisioned in their "mind's eye" when they read the essay. Images include headlines or captions that enlighten a reader of the scrapbook about the relationship between the images, the written prose, and the scrapbook author's vision. This activity leads participants to a better understanding of the emotional power images evoke, particularly the images embedded in written prose. A written commentary explaining each page of the scrapbook documents the scrapbook. The completed scrapbook becomes a memory book containing emotionally moving or theme-centered mini-collages.
- *Materials:* One scrapbook; various magazines from which images can be cut; a collection of creative nonfiction prose essays (e.g., "The Art of the Personal Essay" [Lopate, 1995] or *Short Takes: Brief Encounters with Contemporary Nonfiction* [Kitchen, 2005]); paper and pen; scrapbook supplies such as scissors, glue, paste, tape, glitter, construction paper, markers, plastic page protectors; and computer software such as Broderbund's Print Shop.
- *Suggested time:* Forty to fifty hours
- *Participants:* Individuals or partners
- *Types of learning:* Visual, verbal (written and spoken), physical, intellectual, emotional, spiritual, social, environmental, and reflective

- *Rhetorical forms:* Narration that includes process, information, evaluation, and analysis
- *Prerequisite:* None
- *Precautions:* This activity may require participants to read the essays more than once. Time management should accommodate this possibility.

The Activity

Part 1: Selecting Specific Passages

Highlight passages that are emotionally moving, interesting, or relevant for depicting soul, soil, and society themes.

You will want to use three or four passages in each collage. You may want to select twice as many passages as you need just in case you cannot find images for a particular passage.

Part 2: Finding Images and Creating Captions

This step requires careful time management.

1. Search for pictures and images that integrate the "feeling" of the quote into colors and images.
2. Consider using a software program that lets you create greeting cards, stationary, posters, and so forth, such as Broderbund's Print Shop 20.0, which has over 750,000 images, photos, and templates, all in accordance with the licensing agreement. Be prepared to spend time searching and sorting before selecting. This can become an endless time commitment. Try to set a shorter time limit, three hours perhaps, and see what you get.
3. Be prepared to use an alternative quote if you cannot find an appropriate image to match quotes you first selected.
4. Consider using old magazines or mail-order catalogs.
5. Consider using newspaper headlines when creating captions. Captions should be relevant and show the connections between your vision and the literature or the theme of soul, soil, and society.
6. Consider using old photographs of your own that can be permanently attached in the scrapbook.
7. Consider drawing your own image.
8. Consider creating images out of fabric or use natural materials such as leaves and twigs.

9. There are a lot of ways of creating images. Free your imagination and do something new.

Part 3: Creating the Collage and Compiling the Scrapbook
This step can also be very time consuming. Plan for six to eight hours minimum.

1. You need heavy stock construction paper to hold the images that form each collage.
2. Mat each picture in a unique way that is artistic and beautiful.
3. Supplement each collage with the adjoining quote or caption.
4. You could use clear plastic page protectors for the finished collage.
5. Arrange each collage in an order that makes sense to you.
6. Give your scrapbook an original title.

Part 4: The Written Commentary
The written commentary should include the following parts:

1. A description of the process used when creating the scrapbook
2. Reasons for literary selections
3. Reasons for image selections
4. Reasons for headline or caption selections
5. An analysis of the relationship between images and words
6. A statement that declares what was learned and the degree of satisfaction gained by completing the activity
7. Suggestions for improving the activity

Part 5: Show and Tell
This part is optional, but it is without question a useful part of the activity to include if time allows. People who spend a good amount of time building their scrapbook will want to show it off and talk about how it influenced their understanding of the literature.

Note

1. I am grateful to Carrie Lake, who created a fine scrapbook that featured four short stories and five novels by the American writer Willa Cather. Lake's scrapbook provides superb support for using a holistic approach. When assigned a creative project as a final class project in English 345, Studies in Authors, Lake turned to what she loves to do, scrap booking, as a means of synthesizing her experiences with

the literature. She demonstrated ways students move far beyond the scope of an assignment when they are free to make choices and design the direction of their own learning experience. Lake's written response to the assignment is used here with her permission.

References

Kitchen, J. (Ed.). (2005). *Short takes: Brief encounters with contemporary nonfiction.* New York: Norton.

Lopate, P. (Ed.). (1995). *The art of the personal essay.* New York: Anchor Books.

CHAPTER EIGHTEEN

Voice and Identity

The Sound of Respect

- *Overview*: Participants write a creative nonfiction essay about the quality or development of voice and identity as it is embedded in an expression of respect. Respect can happen in small personal ways or in large universal ways. When we think of respect, we probably first think of respect that is shown by one person for another, but respect can also be demonstrated between large groups of people, nations, ecosystems, financial systems, political systems, religions, biological systems, and so forth. The participants need to select the context, experience, or event within which respect is the primary feature. Soil, soul, and society can easily be interconnected or embedded. Some research to gather truthful facts might be necessary depending on choices made, but personal knowledge alone can also be appropriate.
- *Materials*: The Fourth Genre, by Robert L. Root Jr. and Michael Steinberg (2005); paper and pen; television; radio; and small notebook for keeping notes
- *Suggested time*: To be arranged by the facilitator and participant
- *Participants*: Individuals
- *Types of learning*: Verbal (written and spoken), intellectual, emotional, spiritual, social, environmental, and reflective
- *Rhetorical forms*: Creative nonfiction essay. Possible forms of creative nonfiction to choose from are memoir, nature essay, personal essay, segmented essay, critical essay, and literary journalism.

- *Prerequisite:* An introduction to the fourth literary genre, creative nonfiction. Participants need to be familiar with the various forms of creative nonfiction before starting this activity. To simplify the activity, the facilitator could choose one form and have all participants focus on that one. A more democratic approach would be to introduce all the forms to the participants and let them choose which one to use or vote on whether everyone should use the same form.
- *Precautions:* None

The Activity

Part 1: Points to Remember About Creative Nonfiction

1. The personal presence of the writer is seen or felt in creative nonfiction.[1]
2. Self-discovery and self-exploration are encouraged in creative nonfiction. The form is very flexible and pushes against the boundaries of fiction and poetry. Possible forms of creative nonfiction to choose from are memoir, nature essay, personal essay, segmented essay, critical essay, and literary journalism.
3. Content should be truthful, rather than fictional, to a degree that satisfies the rhetorical purpose of the writing.
4. Autobiography, history, journalism, biology, ecology, travel writing, medicine, and others may offer a framework or subject matter within which the self-exploration or self-discovery is contained.
5. Any literary element that is usually seen in fiction, poetry, and drama can be used when writing a creative nonfiction essay.
6. Creative nonfiction often utilizes the lyrical, dramatic, meditative, expository, and argumentative elements.
7. Innovative or experimental structure is often seen in creative nonfiction. This can include surprising ways of organizing narrative and chronology.
8. Language is literary and imaginative.
9. When writing creative nonfiction, it is helpful to think of the essay as a journey—for the writer and the reader—that leads to a significant point of surprise or discovery.

Part 2: Possible Connections with Soil, Soul, and Society

When selecting a context, experience, or event, mine the soil, soul, and society trinity as a source of inspiration and interconnection. A little brainstorming can offer a start.

Here are a few ideas that could feature soil:

1. animal testing
2. water conservancy
3. land management
4. gardening
5. crop rotation
6. herbicide and pesticide use
7. water treatment plants
8. growing and preserving food

Here are a few ideas that feature soul:

1. joy and personal satisfaction from growing flowers or vegetables
2. respect for a special piece of music that has inspired or soothed
3. donating blood
4. a transcendental moment in nature
5. a challenge nature has imposed that has been overcome
6. an act of kindness or generosity that overwhelms
7. a piece of art that awakens our imaginations
8. a sublime moment of faith in another person

Here are a few ideas drawn from society:

1. ways United Nations members show respect
2. collaboration among businesses that depend on each other for survival, for example, the relationship between trucking and grocery supply
3. the role of respect in a peace negotiation between warring nations
4. the role of respect in union negotiations
5. respect in our judicial system
6. respect in our medical system
7. respect in city council meetings or other governmental decision-making bodies
8. religious tolerance in the United States

Part 3: Finding a Topic and Prewriting Preparation
1. Brainstorm and select a topic.
2. In a sentence or two, identify the level of respect demonstrated by this topic.

3. In a few sentences or questions, attempt to identify the type of voice you want to use or the one you think might be used. Name it and describe its qualities. What do you want to learn about your voice as it functions in relation to this topic?
4. In a few sentences or questions, address identity in the same way you did voice. What do you expect to discover? What would you like to discover?
5. Write a brief passage that describes the interconnections to soil, soul, and society.
6. List all the facts you have about your subject. If you do not have enough, take time to learn more about your topic. Expand your list of facts.

Part 4: Selecting a Form
1. Choose from memoir, nature essay, personal essay, segmented essay, critical essay, and literary journalism.
2. Creative nonfiction often utilizes the lyrical, dramatic, meditative, expository, and argumentative elements.
3. It may be helpful at this point to look at published models of that form, especially if you are trying something for the first time. Refer to *The Fourth Genre* for models.

Part 5: Writing the First Draft
1. Refer to your prewriting preparation as you start.
2. Let your intuition blend with your facts as you shape your essay.
3. Be open to surprises and unexpected discovery.
4. Do not worry so much about form correctness at this stage. Be willing to shift into an alternate form if the essay goes in that direction.
5. Do not aim for any particular length. Let the writing guide that.
6. End the first draft after you have reached a point of satisfaction and discovery is *evident*.

Part 6: Revising the Draft
Check the essay for the following:

1. A point of discovery or surprise is included.
2. The writer's personal presence is felt or heard.
3. Voice and identity are evident, either explicitly or implicitly. An explicit occurrence occurs when voice and identity are part of the topic and are discussed within the essay. An implicit occurrence exists when voice and identity are heard and felt when a reader reads the essay.

4. Connections to soil, soul, and society are included.
5. The form meets the rhetorical conventions inherent in that form but may also be experimental or imaginative.
6. The language is literary and imaginative.
7. The facts are truthful.
8. Literary elements, such as metaphor or figurative language, are used.
9. The essay has something significant to say about the topic.
10. The essay provides readers with a sense of self-discovery or self-exploration.
11. Rewrite where and as often as is necessary or desirable.

Note

1. For this section, see the introduction to *The Fourth Genre* (Root & Steinberg, 2005) for a more detailed discussion of each of these points.

Reference

Root, R. L., Jr., & Steinberg, M. (Eds.). (2005). *The fourth genre: Contemporary writers of/on creative nonfiction* (3rd ed.). New York: Pearson Longman.

CHAPTER NINETEEN

Elements of the Local and Global

Water, Community, and Self

Joy Bracewell

- *Overview*: Participants participate in an online classroom forum, create a journal, and write a reflective letter after exploring water as a practical and metaphoric way of understanding self and community holistically (emotionally, physically, intellectually, socially, aesthetically (beauty), spiritually, and universally). This process facilitates brainstorming within a community space, individual discovery through writing, and composing for a specific audience. Writers will explore the differences in rhetorical strategies and self-expression when publishing information and opinions within a certain character limit electronically, when writing for self and other, and during oral class discussion.
- *Materials*: Computers with Internet access; and writing paper and pen
- *Suggested time*: Time can be determined by the writers and or the facilitator. Time is needed for five parts:

1. Freewriting, reading, and online brainstorming chat
2. Journaling
3. Letter-writing process
4. Reflective meta-writing
5. Class discussion: Nourishing the Self as Local and Global Citizen

- *Types of learning*: Verbal, visual, mental, emotional, physical, spiritual, and social

- *Participants:* Writers
- *Rhetorical forms:* Online forms (140 character limited facts and comments), journaling, and letter-essay
- *Prerequisite:* None. The websites used in this chapter are extremely user-friendly and are easy to navigate even for a first-time user.

The Activity

Part 1: Freewriting, Reading, and Online Brainstorming Chat

1. Each participant should freewrite about water. Let free association or inclination guide your expression; write down the first words that come to your mind.
2. Each participant should then take a few minutes to learn about the "Crisis" in global water using the quick links to infographics and facts at http://water.org.
3. A chat room at http://todaysmeet.com needs to be formed next using a simple name, such as /water123. Students then find the url (e.g., http://todaysmeet.com/water123) and type in the name they would like to use for this session.
4. Students should state their free associations with water and facts they learned from the website, including any insights, surprises, or expectations they may have discovered when writing about water in a nondirected way, reading about it from a global crisis perspective, and sharing perspectives and insights silently, within the character limitations of a chat box.
5. At the end of the chat session, participants in this brainstorming project should begin to shape two or three parameters for personal exploration to chart how they interact with water daily, see it used in their community, or identify its place in the local environment.

Part 2: Journaling

1. Writers decide on a rhetorical structure for each journal entry and how they will record their responses to and interactions with water, such as whether they will include lists, calculations, drawings, maps, photos, and so forth. For written sections, they might choose from classification, narration, description, definition, process analysis, or analysis (see appendix B). Writers may also prefer to use a variety of approaches. Each entry might contain different types of visual and written responses as the daily observations change focus.

2. For their first entry, students also choose a poem about water and compare the speaker's relationship with and actions toward water to their own.
3. Writers identify a rhetorical aim for each entry (persuasive, informative, or expressive; see appendix B).
4. To prepare for the last journal entry, writers watch videos featuring a named participant in the Water.org program under Recent Posts and learn as much as possible about the customs and language of that person's country. Then they report on how the journaling and noticing process has affected their relationship to understanding their selves within the environment and in relation to local and global communities.

Part 3: Letter Writing
1. Use your experience with prewriting, reading and online classroom chat, and journaling as you compose a letter to the person featured in the Water.org video in which you consider the connections you both have to water.
2. Think about what you know about this person based on what you can see and hear in the video and what you do not know due to the limitations of this mode of communication. Assuming that this person will be able to comprehend your letter through a translator or other means, think about what you can and cannot convey to him or her using written language. Include a visual of some kind to supplement your message.

Part 4: Reflective Meta-Writing
Attach a paragraph that addresses the following elements in your letter:

- Audience
- Aim
- Purpose
- Rationale for visual
- What was omitted or changed from previous drafts
- What the writers like about their essay
- What the writers don't like about their essay
- A comment about prewriting activities that explains to what degree the activities were helpful

Part 5: Class Discussion: Nourishing the Self as Local and Global Citizen

For Classroom Formats

The teacher or facilitator can initiate a group discussion that invites writers to

1. share what they learned about how they participate in online communities in comparison to traditional classroom discussions;
2. share what they learned about how their expression changes for collaborative brainstorming versus individual writing;
3. discuss their aesthetic response to water or disease;
4. discuss the writing process;
5. discuss their emotions about any of the above;
6. suggest ways of improving the activities; and
7. give reasons they may or may not feel a stronger sense of awareness and belonging as local and global citizens.

For Continued Action

Writers might want to start a fund-raising campaign and revise their previous writing to compose e-mails and posts that will convey to friends, family, and local, global, and virtual community members how their experiences shaped their understanding of themselves and the importance of clean water worldwide. Or they may want to have a conversation about their experiences with someone who has lived through changes to the water delivery system in their area. Another alternative would be to find a pen pal in a country affected by water shortages to find out about that person and share experiences.

CHAPTER TWENTY

Writing the Outdoors

Three Days in Nature

- *Overview:* An extended three-day (or longer) gathering can occur during a camping trip or at a lodge resort if camping is undesirable to the participants. It is essential to select a site that is accessible to nature. This site can be local or at a distance. The learning purposes of each group help determine site location. Why is there a minimum of three days? An extended time together offers multiple opportunities for holistic educational experiences and can be shaped to meet the special interests of the participants. The trinity of soil, soul, and society automatically and naturally arises. Preparation, planning, and cost can be shared by all the participants. The main intention of this three-day outdoor learning activity is to introduce the participants to basic attitudes and beliefs about the environment and their connection to it that they may not have yet considered.
- *Materials:* Determined by site qualities and activities selected during preevent preparation
- *Suggested time:* Friday through Sunday or three consecutive weekdays
- *Participants:* Groups
- *Types of learning:* Verbal (written and spoken), auditory, visual, intellectual, emotional, spiritual, social, environmental, and reflective
- *Rhetorical forms:* Journal writing and other types as determined by the participants
- *Prerequisite:* Extensive preparation; possibly fundraising. It is imperative that the group facilitator have environmental or ecological knowledge

and be able to share that knowledge with group participants, because learners are likely to remember knowledge and learn faster from a mentor. The group facilitator may retain the role of knowledge seeker and learner but should in some way be more knowledgeable than the group participants, especially if a long-term change in attitude and behavior is a purpose.
- *Precautions:* Poll participants for information such as allergies, personal preferences, and so forth. Other precautions are determined by site qualities and previous outdoor experience of the participants. For instance, during white-water rafting everyone should have a life preserver and helmet, or when camping during summer those allergic to bee stings should carry medication and inform the group facilitator of their allergy ahead of time in case a bee sting occurs. A list of precautions should be generated *before* the event takes place. A three-day outdoor learning experience is not for everyone, and no person should be forced to go along. *An alternative to the activity should be offered by the facilitator or created and suggested by the participant.*

The Activity

Why Outdoor Learning?

The extensive literature on outdoor learning is generally divided into adventure education and environmental education. Adventure education places students into some level of real or perceived risk so that when they successfully meet challenges they experience growth. Environmental education provides knowledge about and experiences in nature as a means to change people into ecological stewards and activists.

Research by Glenda Hanna and others indicate that "recreational experiences play an important role in influencing higher levels of environmental concern and activism" (1995, p. 22). Today it is generally accepted that providing children and young adults with direct experiences in nature lead to a stronger appreciation and understanding of ecology.

Moreover, a study reported by Hanna indicates "that it is important to develop a positive, ecocentric wilderness attitude through cognitive channels as well as through affective and physical channels" (1995, p. 29). In other words, a holistic approach to learning the outdoors by being in the outdoors has greater impact on learners than does classroom experience alone.

When learners have direct contact with the outdoors, something magical happens for many of them. They develop a new sense of awe and wonder about the planet earth and about their relationship with it. They begin to recognize the power of place and the way place shapes personal and cultural identity. They have the opportunity to change attitudes and behaviors about the earth and about how its resources are used. Learners awaken in dramatic, at times sublime, ways that reconnect them to beauty and to life. They may awaken to self and spirit.

Not all learners have a dramatic or spiritual awakening in nature. Participants who have internalized a competitive, consumerist approach to life may have difficulty observing the subtle beauty that is in nature. The "drama" in nature may not be as loud or as fast as an action film at their local theater. Some people prefer shopping trips and fast-food eateries and have difficulty adjusting to a new set of challenges, particularly those designed by nature.

Pretrip preparation can establish realistic expectations for those who are not so inclined to feel "comfortable" in nature. It is part of the facilitator's role to discuss the ups and downs of outdoor learning and to begin building a sense of community so that, if it becomes necessary, an uncomfortable participant knows whom to turn to for support. The facilitator needs to bring the participants to accept the idea that education is not simply something than happens indoors.

According to Laura Parker Roerden, "Fewer than 10 percent of our children in the United States today learn about nature by being in nature. More than half learn about the natural world through technology and the rest from inside a classroom" (2001, p. 60). Her attempts to teach science through an extensive scuba diving field trip has met with success and significantly changed students as it has changed her. She testifies that

> when you teach outside, what I think of as a "third presence" emerges, guiding and informing the learning—the earth itself will seemingly have a voice. When I've surrendered to this feeling, I've noticed my own passions reawakened. I've found the job of being all-knowing teacher impossible—nature reveals herself as too complex. Mysteries I do not yet understand reengage me as a learner. My sense of wonder and curiosity is renewed. Nature is not only the classroom; it is the teacher. The earth protects us, nurtures us, tells us about the shape of our heart, and we in kind are called to do the same for the earth. (2001, p. 63)

As David Orr tells us, the goal of ecological literacy "is not just a comprehension of how the world works, but in the light of that knowledge, a life lived accordingly" (1992, p. 87). Orr further tells us that there are some common elements shared among those who are more comfortable with the environment: experience in the natural world at an early age; the presence of an older teacher or mentor as a role model; and seminal books that explain, heighten, and say what we have felt deeply (1992, p. 88). The facilitation of an outdoor learning activity can be grounded by establishing experience with these common elements.

Part 1: Intention and Purpose

Early preparation for any outdoor learning experience requires specific decisions and time allowances that prepare the facilitator(s) and the participants.

1. A clear intention for the trip should be articulated. Will it be an "adventure" or "environmental" educational experience? Or can the trip be designed in a way to accommodate both adventure and environmental education?
2. In what way are the participants challenged?
3. What are participants expected to learn?
4. How might they change, and is change short term or long term?
5. How might change be recognized or measured?

Part 2: Date and Site Selection

The time of year for the three-day adventure and specific site qualities will determine the sorts of equipment needed as well as the direction or focus the learning experiences might take.

The participants need to select a weekend date before selecting a site. When reserving space, the exact dates are needed. If the group is free to go during the week, campground and resort rates are often lower.

Pros and Cons

Springtime is milder with fewer bugs. Usually spring is considered "preseason" and rates are often lower. Sites are generally in less demand and therefore less crowded. The weather can be unpredictable, rainy, cold, or cloudy. Water temperature in lakes and rivers is colder, even icy in certain parts of the country or at high altitudes. Hiking and biking trails can be muddy or impassable. Nights are cooler. Pollens can be uncomfortable for those with asthma or hay fever.

Summer months provide the most predictable weather. Bugs can be a nuisance. Rates are at the highest. Water temperature is usually warm enough for swimming or other water activities. Trails are generally well groomed and accessible. Nights are warmer. Pollens can be higher and uncomfortable for those with asthma or hay fever.

Fall months are generally drier than spring and offer warm days and cool, even crisp nights. Rates may be lower than during summer months but still a bit higher than during spring. Trails are still accessible. Bugs such as mosquitoes or flies are less problematic. Pollens have generally calmed down, but leaf mold can be a problem for those with allergies.

Winter months are colder. Travel can be hazardous and unpredictable. Campers can be at risk even with the right equipment if a storm comes on. Rates are low and sites are generally empty or under-utilized. Bugs are gone. There are fewer daylight hours. The challenge to survive offers a higher level of success and satisfaction. Trails are often inaccessible except by snowshoes or skis. Lakes and rivers can be frozen.

The participants need to select a wilderness location. Longer travel time means less site time and higher expense. A location not more than four hours (by car) from home is reasonable.

The participants need to decide if they want to camp and if so what sort of camping. For example, will they backpack to a more remote spot, or will they car camp (vehicles are parked next to campsite). Will they tent camp or camp in recreational vehicles? Will they camp in a county park or a state park? Will the campground offer flush toilets and showers or pit toilets? Will the campground offer electricity for recreational vehicles? Most states have an 800 number for state campground reservations. Most county parks do not require or accept reservations and offer space on a first-come basis.

Pros and Cons

Tent camping or backpacking requires sleeping on the ground, setting up a tent, and cooking over an open fire or camp stove. The biggest advantage (or disadvantage, depending on point of view) to this type of adventure is that participants are out of doors *all of the time*. Even when sleeping in a tent, there is a sense of being outdoors because there are not four walls and a roof or floor.

Naturally, weather conditions can cause interesting challenges, to say the least. The ability to stay warm and dry is important as is the availability of drinking water and personal hygiene options. After being out of doors for an extended time period, some participants may have difficulty reassimilating to indoor living after the trip.

The participants need to decide if they would prefer an adventure weekend at a resort lodge, rather than a campout experience. All across the country there are resorts and lodges for daily, weekend, weekly, and even monthly rental. Most come fully equipped with bedding, kitchens, bathrooms, fireplaces, firewood, and the like. The extent of amenities is usually included in the property descriptions, and if something is lacking it often can be negotiated. Some places give discount prices during off seasons and or for educational groups.

Pros and Cons

Protection from bad weather is the strongest advantage, but others include beds, showers, flush toilets, kitchen facilities, heat, running water, and various amenities one associates with a hotel or home. If weather is bad, it also might mean that everyone is reluctant to go out of doors, and if there are too many people for the space, nerves can get stretched. Noise levels may also get too high, and privacy may be harder to find. Participants need to be more assertive about being in nature and mini-lessons that require outdoor learning need to be facilitated. A resort or lodge is usually more expensive.

Part 3: Types of Possible Trips

As part of the planning process, participants can brainstorm about the type of trip that appeals to them and that is also feasible. The type of trip that is finally selected should interconnect with dates and site selection. A few suggestions are listed below:

- An adventure of identity and sharing: a three-day focus on knowing the terrain and each other
- Apple picking
- Bird sanctuaries
- Canoeing a local river
- Harvest time at an organic farm
- Historic forts
- Mountain hiking
- Native American powwows or festivals
- Planting time at an organic farm
- A reader's weekend: share your favorite book and author
- River rafting
- Searching the sky for star constellations
- Service work in a near distant community
- Silent retreat in the country
- Ski trips
- Tent camping
- Visiting a virgin forest
- Visiting the birthplace of a famous author, musician, or painter
- Wildlife preserve
- A writer's weekend: time to write

Find and select a focus, a purpose, one that suits the particular group of participants.

Part 4: Funding the Trip
A number of funding options exist.

1. Participants equally share the total cost.
2. Donations are requested from local organizations such as the Moose, Elk, or Rotary Club.
3. Sponsors are secured from among local businesses.
4. Donations for funds are made from local churches.
5. Schools sometimes have "field trip" funds set aside.
6. Funding is requested from parents or other relatives.
7. Specific fundraising projects, such as car washes, yard work, bake sales, and bottle drives, are conducted by the participants.

Anyone wishing to participate should not be turned away due to cost.

Part 5: Identify Special Needs
There are usually special needs attached to any group. These need to be identified and a plan put into place to accommodate them *before* arriving at the destination.

Part 6: Gathering the Food
The amount and types of food are determined by the number in the group as well as by the type of adventure the group has selected. If refrigeration is lacking, coolers and ice may be necessary, but when backpacking, coolers and ice are not an option. Some resorts or lodges also provide meals. First, it is necessary to select a site and type of adventure before identifying and securing food needs. Once the group has reached that point, the following process can help:

List all meals, for example,

- Friday, dinner
- Friday, snack
- Saturday, breakfast
- Saturday, lunch
- Saturday, dinner
- Saturday, snack
- Sunday, breakfast

- Sunday, lunch
- Sunday, return road trip snacks

List special needs, for example,
- Number of vegetarians
- Types of food allergies
- Alternatives to foods like milk or cheese for those who need them
- Meat alternatives for vegetarians

1. Prepare menus for each meal.
2. Determine quantity needed.
3. Equally share the responsibility of providing the food.
4. Estimate cost of food and add this to the total trip cost.

Part 7: Equipment Lists
The equipment that is brought along is partially determined by the type of trip that is chosen. The process below can help:

1. Make a complete list of equipment that is needed.
2. Create two categories: individual and group need.
3. Let each individual meet their own need for individual items, such as toothbrush and sleeping bag.
4. Share the responsibility for providing the other pieces of equipment that become "communal equipment," such as camp stove, three coolers, three frying pans, and matches. Identify who brings each item.

Part 8: Extended Invitations
Certain age groups need additional attention, especially when it is a mixed-gender group. Extending invitation to others can help meet these needs. Consider inviting

- parents,
- grandparents,
- neighbors,
- older siblings, and
- other adult facilitators.

Once extended invitations have been accepted, a group meeting to name and agree to certain behavioral policies is helpful. It sets boundaries and lets people know ahead of time what can happen if these boundaries are trespassed.

Part 9: Liability Issues
Liability issues exist for all age groups, but particular issues exist for underage participants. The facilitator needs to consider the following:

1. Parental or guardian permission forms
2. Transportation insurance
3. Accident insurance
4. Procedures to use if needed. For example, if the lead facilitator is called away to the hospital with an injured participant, the facilitator's replacement selected ahead of time can cut down on stress during a crisis. The group can identify such procedures during the general meeting about expected behavioral policies.

Part 10: Suggestions for Writing Activities
The writing activities can also be determined by the participants; perhaps one group wants to write intensively, while another group wants to keep writing to a minimum. At the very least, participants should bring journals for an amount of daily writing they self-select. Other activities might include the following:

- Collaborative writing
- Creative writing
- Evaluation recommendations at the end of the adventure trip
- Guided mini-lessons
- Letters to relatives or friends
- Nature writing
- Poetry workshop
- Reflections on the unfamiliar
- Responses to others' writing
- Responses to reading selections

The level of significance in any activity is difficult to determine until *after* the experience is completed. Even the smallest activity can become imbued with the power to transform perception and to initiate deeper meaning when the participant is ready to receive the gifts inherent in the activity.

Part 11: Nonwriting Activities to Stimulate Writing
As part of preevent preparation, participants or the facilitator can select and design nonwriting activities that are meant to stimulate on-site writing.[1] A few suggestions are listed below:

- Analysis of group dynamics
- Cooking for a larger group of people
- Creating a catalog of trees on-site
- Edible food indigenous to the area, for example, chamomile, mint, berries, or specific mushrooms
- Fishing
- Listing indigenous wildlife, birds, or insects
- Observation of animal tracks that were identified during a preevent mini-lesson
- Observation of star constellations
- Silent time
- Swimming
- Water testing of a nearby river, brook, or lake
- Yoga practice

Just about any activity during the event can be a subject for writing. Simply sitting quietly in one spot to observe the activity over a complete hour can be produce interesting observations and reflections for writing journal entries, songs, poems, letters, and nonfiction.

Note

1. A friend and colleague, Don Backus, told me of a meaningful outdoor activity he was assigned. The instructor took students to a nearby wooded area and placed them here and about but well spaced apart from each other. Each student was told not to move and to rope off a one-square-foot area. They then observed all life occurring within that one square foot. Don said his awareness of the existing diversity within that small space led him to understand the sensitive but strong balance between ecosystems found in the woods *and* that led him to reconsider interconnections upon which larger systems are built. Years after he had this experience, he still referred to it as one of his most meaningful educational experiences.

References

Bowers, C. A. (1995). The cultural dimensions of ecological literacy. *Journal of Environmental Education, 27*, 5–10.

Hanna, G. (1995). Wilderness-related environmental outcomes of adventure and ecology educational programing. *Journal of Environmental Education, 27,* 21–32.

Orr, D. (1992). *Ecological literacy: Education and the transition to a postmodern world.* Albany: State University of New York Press.

Roerden, L. P. (2001). Lessons of the wild. In L. Lantieri (Ed.), *Schools with spirit* (pp. 53–76). Boston: Beacon.

Appendix A

Interesting Schools

- Academy at Swift River
  www.academyatswiftriver.crchealth.com
- Albany Free School
  www.albanyfreeschool.org
- Alger Learning Center/Independence High School
  www.independent-learning.com
- Alpine Valley School
  www.alpinevalleyschool.com
- Austin Waldorf School
  www.austinwaldorf.org
- The Bay School
  www.bayschool.org
- The Beach School Toronto, Ontario
  www.thebeachschool.org
- Berkeley Montessori School in Berkeley, California
  www.theberkeleyschool.org
- Blue Mountain School, Cottage Grove, Oregon
  www.greatschools.org/oregon/cottage-grove
- Brockwood Park School (UK)
  www.brockwood.org.uk
- Burke Mountain Academy, East Burke, Vermont
  www.burkemtnacademy.org

- Cape Byron Rudolf Steiner School, Byron Bay, Australia
  www.capebyronsteiner.nsw.edu.au
- Cedarwood Sudbury School
  www.greatschools.org
- Christian Montessori School of Ann Arbor, Michigan
  www.cmsaa.org
- The Circle School, Harrisburg, Virginia
  www.circleschool.org
- Clonlara Campus School
  www.clonlara.org/campus.htm
- Daycroft Montessori School
  www.daycroft.org
- The Detroit Waldorf School, Detroit, Michigan
  www.detroitwaldorf.com
- Ephraim Curtis Middle School
  www.sudbury.k12.ma.us/curtis/about.html
- Evergreen Community Charter School
  www.evergreenccs.org
- Exinox Holistic Alternative School, Toronto
  www.wholechild.school.ca
- Follow the Child (Montessori), Raleigh, North Carolina
  www.followthechild.org
- The Friends School of Minnesota
  www.fsm.org
- The Gap State High School, Australia
  www.thegapshs.eq.edu.au
- Greenwood Sudbury School in Hampton, Connecticut
  www.greatschools.org
- Grove School
  www.groveschool.org
- Jefferson County Open School
  www.jeffcoopen.org
- The Kino School
  www.kinoschool.org
- Knoxville Montessori School
  www.meadmontessorischool.com
- The Learning Exchange
  www.learningexchange.org
- The Liberty School
  www.thelibertyschool.org

- The Living School
  www.thelivingschool.org
- Marin Day Schools in Mill Valley, California
  www.marindayschools.org
- The Meeting School, Rindge, New Hampshire
  www.meetingschool.org
- Middlesex School
  www.mxschool.edu
- The New School
  www.tnsk.org
- The New School of Monmouth County
  www.the-new-school.com
- The New School of Northern Virginia
  www.newschoolva.com
- North Star Center, Hadley Massachusetts
  www.northstarteens.org
- Oak Grove School
  www.oakgroveschool.com
- Oakland Steiner School
  www.oaklandsteiner.org
- Park Day School in Oakland, California
  www.parkdayschool.org
- Play Mountain Place
  www.playmountain.org
- Puget Sound Community School
  www.pscs.org
- Rainbow Mountain Children's School, Asheville, North Carolina
  www.rmcs.org
- Reston Montessori School
  www.montessori.com
- The Rudolph Steiner School of South Devon, UK
  www.steiner-south-devon.org
- Saklan Valley School
  www.saklan.org
- San Francisco Waldorf School
  www.sfwaldorf.org
- The Scarsdale Alternative School
  www.scarsdaleschools.org
- The School of Total Education, Warwick, Queensland, Australia
  www.sote.qld.edu.au/about/keyfacts.html

- The Second Foundation School
  www.secondfoundationschool.com
- The Steiner School at Middle Wood, Roeburndale West, Lancaster, UK
  www.lancastersteiner.orgupk
- Stepping Stones, Grand Rapids, Michigan
  www.steppingstonesgr.org
- Stone Mountain School in Black Mountain, North Carolina
  www.stonemountainschool.com
- St. Paul's School
  www.sps.edu
- Tamariki School, Christchurch, New Zealand
  www.tamariki.chch.saschchoolzone.net.nz
- Tierra Pacifica Charter School
  www.tierrapacifica.org
- The Tutorial School
  www.tutorialschool.org
- Upattinas School and Resource Center, Glenmore, Pennsylvania
  www.upattinas.org
- Verde Valley School, Sedona Arizona
  www.vvsaz.org
- The Woolman Semester
  www.woolman.org
- Yaxche Learning Center
  www.yaxche.org

Higher Education

- Antioch College
  www.antioch.org
- Bennington College
  www.bennington.edu
- California State University, San Bernardino
  MA in education; holistic and integrative education option
  www.csusb.edu/coe/programs/holstic_integed/index.htm
- Earlham College
  www.earlham.edu
- Fairhaven College
  www.wwu.edu/fairhaven
- The International Foundation for Holistic Education
  www.ramongallegos.com

-
- Maharishi University of Management
  www.mum.edu
- Naropa University
  www.naropa.edu
- The New School
  www.newschool.edu
- Schumacher College
  www.schumachercolege.org.uk

Appendix B
Rhetorical Aims and Organizational Strategies

Aims

1. The *argumentative* aim seeks to convince someone to accept your point of view or beliefs about a particular idea or issue.[1] It relies on logical factual information and almost always omits any reference to emotions or anecdotal information. When emotional information is used, it is then referred to as the persuasive aim because it is generally held to persuade, while facts and logic are objective evidence that leads to readers changing their position to those presented in the argument. In practice, argumentation and persuasion often become synonymous.
2. The *informative aim* provides information to the reader. It is most often used in reports and relies on explanations of facts. It omits arguments and opinions.
3. The *expressive aim* shows the writer's emotions. The writer's personal point of view directs the writing. Expressive writing is most often used in autobiography and in creative nonfiction.

Organizational Strategies

(Also referred to as rhetorical modes)

1. *Definition* writing offers detailed information that defines. The focus can be on a single word, an idea, an issue, a person, or a place. Definition relies on facts, and in some cases can include the writer's personal

opinion. Depending on the topic, definition can be purely objective or subjective. The concept government, for example, can be formally defined by looking at facts and types of governments people use; it can also be informally defined by describing what it means to the writer on a personal basis.
2. When using *illustration*, writers provide examples to "illustrate" or demonstrate their point.
3. *Classification* requires grouping together ideas, issues, or objects that are the same or very similar. For example, when discussing flowers, those that grow year after year without any new planting are classed as "perennials" whereas those flowers that must be planted anew each spring or fall are classed as "annuals." Edible parts of vegetables that grow underground like carrots, potatoes, or onions are classed as "root vegetables." Writers identify the elements or characteristics that qualify their subject for one group or another.
4. When *description* is used in writing, writers choose to reveal how subjects look, feel, sound, and function in terms of their relationship in space.
5. *Comparison contrast* is used when writers want to demonstrate how things are the same or how they are different. When writers compare two things, they look for the characteristics in each that are the same, and when they contrast those two things they look for characteristics that are different.
6. *Process analysis*. There are three types of process analysis: writing the steps down about how a person did something; writing the steps down about how another person did something; and writing the steps down about how to do something. Process writing almost always involves step-by-step actions or instructions to be taken.
7. In *analysis* writing, writers look at the parts of the whole in order to understand or make meaning about the whole. Analysis requires looking very closely at the parts and their relationship to one another as well as to how they come together to make the whole.

Note

1. Expanded versions of the information in this appendix can be found in nearly every grammar handbook on the market.

Annotated Bibliography

Abra, J. (1997). *The motives for creative work*. Cresskill, NJ: Hampton Press. A fundamental orientation to the psychology of creativity is presented. Motivation, drive, competition, biological, and environmental sources are analyzed.

Amabile, T. M. (1983). *The social psychology of creativity*. New York: Springer-Verlag. An important scholarly study of intrinsic motivations in creativity studies.

Ashton-Warner, S. (1986). *Teacher*. New York: Simon & Schuster. Ashton-Warner describes an innovative teaching process she used with Maori students in New Zealand. Creativity becomes the agent of change.

Bachelard, G. (1969). *The poetics of space*. Boston: Beacon. A phenomenological study of space and ways it governs perspective.

Boden, M. A. (Ed.). (1994). *Dimensions of creativity*. Cambridge, MA: MIT Press. A scholarly collection of essays that explore creativity studies.

Bopp, J., Bopp, M., Brown, L., & Lane, P. (1984). *The sacred tree*. Alberta, Canada: Four Worlds Development Press. A detailed presentation of various ways to understand and use the medicine wheel in daily life.

Bowers, C. A. (1995). The cultural dimensions of ecological literacy. *Journal of Environmental Education, 27*, 5–10. This opinion piece offers a critical perspective of David Orr's definitions and for ecological literacy. Bowers contextualizes definitions and understandings within a cultural episteme.

Brand, A. G., & Graves, R. L. (Eds.). (1994). *Presence of mind: Writing and the domain beyond the cognitive*. Portsmouth, NH: Boynton Cook. A collection of essays written by scholars in education and composition studies. These authors explore a range of innovate approaches to teaching writing that address the whole learner, multiple intelligences, and holistic ways of learning.

Carpenter, R. (2011). *Awakening: 12 tools to unlock ultimate potential.* Murfreesboro, TN: Cultivation Network. Twelve chapters describe individual tools and offer exercises that promise self-development. These tools are as follows: defining who you are, what you want, and how you feel; deep listening; standing in your power; the need to be right; silence and stillness; looking prejudice in the eye; completing the past; organization and time management; living foods; living out your passions and purpose; declaring your future; and original pain/inner child work.

Crowell, S., & Reid-Marr, D. (2013). *Emergent teaching: A path of creativity, significance and transformation.* Lanham, MD: Rowman & Littlefield Education. Moving away from the emergent learning in students that is associated with Reggio Emilia curriculum, the authors present a pedagogy based on spontaneity and "occasions" that naturally arise in teaching moments. With a focus on the teacher, emergent teaching "is a different way of perceiving our roles as teachers. It includes engagement, playful discovery, deep inquiry, and creativity."

Dallaire, Michael. (2011). *Teaching with the wind: Spirituality in Canadian education.* Lanham, MD: University Press of America. Dallaire provides a contemplative voice about the positive aspects of a spiritual approach to education. While the book is aimed at Canadians, there is much that will appeal to educators anywhere who seek practical guidance and concrete examples.

Foehr, R. F., & Schiller, S. A. (Eds.). (1997). *The spiritual side of writing: Releasing the learner's whole potential.* Portsmouth, NH: Heinemann Boynton Cook. The first full collection of essays within composition studies that explore spiritual approaches to writing. Philosophical and pedagogical information is included.

Gardner, H. (1983). *Frames of mind.* New York: Basic. Gardner presents his theory and model of seven intelligences.

Gardner, H. (1994). The creators' patterns. In M. A. Boden (Ed.), *Dimensions of creativity* (pp. 143–158). Cambridge, MA: MIT Press. Gardner overviews creativity studies, provides a definition of creativity, and uses seven cases (Freud, Einstein, Picasso, Stravinsky, Eliot, Graham, and Gandhi) that examine creative processes. A fuller view of these case studies is detailed in Gardner's 1993 book *The Creators of the Modern Era.*

Gifford, D. (1956). The creative process in the classroom. Paper presented at Conference on Creativity as a Process. Arden House, Harriman, NY, October 10–12. Gifford describes ways the creative process is evoked in classroom teaching.

Goleman, D. (1995). *Emotional intelligence.* New York: Bantam Books. Goleman breaks new ground by defining and describing emotional intelligence. He makes an effective case for why it can be more important than IQ.

Goleman, D., Kaufman, P., & Ray, M. (1992). *The creative spirit.* New York: Dutton/Penguin. Inspired by the television show *The Creative Spirit,* this book persuades readers to believe that the creative spirit is in all of us and that a widespread creative renaissance is possible if people let the creative spirit infuse their lives.

Goswami, A., & Goswami, M. (1999). *Quantum creativity: Waking up to our creative potential.* Cresskill, NJ: Hampton Press. This book suggests that consciousness is the central theme of the universe and that "creativity is our lifeline to consciousness" (xv). It provides an integrated approach to all the various forms of creativity and looks closely at ways all people of all ages can realize their creative potential.

Greenberg, D. (1987). *Free at last: The Sudbury Valley School.* Framingham, MA: Sudbury Valley School Press. Greenberg, teacher at Sudbury, writes a personal and descriptive overview of the first Sudbury School.

Hanna, G. (1995). Wilderness-related environmental outcomes of adventure and ecology educational programing. *Journal of Environmental Education, 27,* 21–32. This longitudinal research uses qualitative and quantitative measures to compare and contrast adventure education and ecology education programs. It suggests support for a holistic approach to bring about long-term change.

Harrison, S. (2002). *The happy child.* Boulder, CO: Sentient Publications. This book declares that education needs to be aimed at preserving and responding to the child's happiness. It criticizes the climate of competition and fear that prevails in compulsory and public education and supports developing community-based learning communities.

Juergensmeyer, M. (1984). *Gandhi's way: A handbook of conflict resolution.* Berkeley: University of California Press. Juergensmeyer presents an overview of Gandhian theory and practice as well as case study results and solutions to some difficulties existing in the Gandhi approach to conflict resolution.

Kane, J. (2002). Waldorf education: Reflections on the essentials. In J. P. Miller & Y. Nakagawa (Eds.), *Nurturing our wholeness: Perspectives on spirituality in education* (pp. 241–263). Brandon, VT: Foundation for Educational Renewal. Kane writes a thorough and detailed review of Waldorf education.

Kessler, R. (2000). *The soul of education.* Alexandria, VA: Association for Supervision and Curriculum Development. This book presents seven gateways through which students might pass as a means to nourish soul and to stimulate the whole person. It presents a holistic model and calls for education reform at the local and national levels.

Kitchen, J. (Ed.). (2005). *Short takes: Brief encounters with contemporary nonfiction.* New York: Norton. This collection features short contemporary essays that suit limited reading times.

Kumar, S. (2002). *You are therefore I am: A declaration of dependence.* Devon, UK: Green Books. This book presents the spiritual journey of the author and presents a spiritual, philosophical, and practical view of holism that any person can use for daily living.

Lantieri, L. (Ed.). (2001). *Schools with spirit: Nurturing the inner lives of children and teachers.* Boston: Beacon. An excellent collection of essays focused on spiritual approaches to learning. A broad and nonreligious perspective dominates the work and invites an acceptance of spirit in schools.

Lantieri, L., & Patti, J. (1996). *Waging peace in our schools.* Boston: Beacon. Peacekeeping and violence-prevention strategies and processes that have proven effective in schools are documented and supported by specific cases.

Lopate, P. (Ed.). (1995). *The art of the personal essay.* New York: Anchor Books. This seminal collection features a broad range of essays that are organized by topic and genre.

McMahan, E., Funk R., & Day, S. (1988). *The elements of writing about literature and film.* New York: Macmillan. A brief overview of literary elements used in literature and film. Includes chapters on fiction, poetry, drama, and the writing process, and a glossary of definitions.

Mercogliano, C. (1998). *Making it up as we go along: The story of the Albany Free School.* Portsmouth, NH: Heinemann. This book provides philosophy, history, and practice of a democratic approach to education as it is practiced at the Albany Free School. It offers alternatives to conventional mainstream education.

Meyers, P. (2003). K2. In J. Standord (Ed.), *Responding to literature: Stories, poems, plays and essays* (pp. 891–913, 4th ed.) Boston: McGraw Hill. Two men, one injured, are trapped on a mountain at twenty-seven thousand feet. An argument follows as to why the able-bodied man should leave his friend alone to die.

Michalko, M. (2001). *Cracking creativity: The secrets of creative genius.* Berkeley, CA: Ten Speed Press. This book provides a variety of practical and easy-to-use strategies for developing creativity in individuals.

Miller, J. P. (1993). *Holistic teacher.* Toronto: Ontario Institute for Studies in Education Press. Offers guidelines and philosophy for becoming a holistic teacher.

Miller, J. P. (1996). *The holistic curriculum.* Toronto: Ontario Institute for Studies in Education Press. An introduction to what a holistic curriculum contains and how it is facilitated. Theoretical and philosophical foundations are also provided.

Miller, J. P. (2000). *Education and the soul.* Albany, NY: State University of New York Press. The first half presents historical and philosophical frames for addressing the soul in education. The second half describes practices a teacher might use in the classroom. This book is drawn from Miller's long career in holistic teaching.

Miller, J. P. (2006). *Educating for wisdom and compassion.* Thousand Oaks, CA: Corwin. Theoretical and philosophical foundations, practice, and outcomes of this approach are described by Miller.

Miller, J. P. (2010). *Whole child education.* Toronto: University of Toronto Press. Educating the whole school through a model of transmission, transaction, and transformation is espoused. Practical examples from Exinox Holistic Alternative School (formerly Toronto's Whole Child School) are included.

Miller, J. P., & Nakagawa, Y. (2002). *Nurturing our wholeness: Perspectives on spirituality in education.* Brandon VT: Foundation for Educational Renewal. A collection of essays that addresses traditions, teachers, and practices. This book broadens the discussion about secular spirituality in education.

Miller, J. P., et al. (Eds.). (2005). *Holistic learning and spirituality in education.* Albany, NY: State University of New York Press. This collection of essays is based on conference presentations from the first three International Holistic Education Conferences held in Toronto every two years.

Miller, R. (1991). *New directions in education: Selections from Holistic Review.* Brandon, VT: Holistic Education Press. This collection includes over thirty essays that were previously published in the journal *Holistic Education Review.* A broad range of topics articulating and demonstrating holistic principles are covered.

Miller, R. (1997). *What are schools for? Holistic education in American culture* (3rd rev. ed.). Brandon, VT: Holistic Education Press. Political, philosophical, social, financial, cultural, and historical pressures that have caused holistic education to emerge are thoroughly presented. This book provides an excellent starting point and introduction to the field of holistic education.

Miller, R. (Ed.). (2000). *Creating learning communities: Models, resources, and new ways of thinking about teaching and learning.* Brandon, VT: Foundation for Educational Renewal. This is an excellent introduction to alternative educational choices such as homeschooling and community learning centers.

Mintz, J., Solomon, R., & Solomon, S. (Eds.). (1994). *The handbook of alternative education.* New York: Macmillan. This is a resource directory that lists alternative schools. The first thirty pages describe and orient readers to alternative education. Four classifications include public choice, public at risk, independent (or private), and home based.

Moffett, J. (1994). *The universal schoolhouse: Spiritual awakening through education.* San Francisco: Jossey-Bass. One of the first full-length discussions about spiritual approaches in education.

Neill, A. S. (1992). *Summerhill school: A new view of childhood.* Albert Lamb (Ed.). New York: St. Martin's Griffin. Summerhill school established the traditions associated with the "free school." It is the model from which many free schools arose. This book describes Summerhill and the people credited with beginning a revolutionary form of education.

Neville, B. (1989). *Educating psyche.* North Blackburn, Australia: Collins Dove. Neville persuades readers to reconstruct their view of education so that it moves beyond logic and rationality as primary teaching methods. Readers are encouraged to use autosuggestion, visualization, positive affirmation, constructive imagining, the power of myths, metaphors, meditation, the relaxation response, and others.

Newberg, A., & Waldman, M. R. (2010). *How God changes your brain.* New York: Ballantine. Breakthrough findings from neuroscience support various meditation practices as a way to strengthen mental, physical, and spiritual health. The authors make a compelling case for integrating meditation in daily life, including in education.

Noddings, N. (1992). *The challenge to care in schools: An alternative approach to education.* New York: Teachers College Press. Noddings presents a philosophy of "care" as a framework for educational reform. People learn best in an environment of caring that is based on support rather than on competition or evaluation.

Orr, D. (1992). *Ecological literacy: Education and the transition to a postmodern world.* Albany: State University of New York Press. A seminal book that defines ecological literacy and offers theory and practice to encourage ecological literacy.

Palmer, P. J. (1998). *The courage to teach: Exploring the inner landscape of a teacher's life*. San Francisco: Jossey-Bass. An exploration of why teachers teach and on why personal rejuvenation and professional development must come from the heart.

Rocha, D. L. D. (2003). *Schools where children matter: Exploring educational alternatives*. Brandon, VT: Foundation for Educational Renewal. Three holistic schools are profiled with praise and criticism. Parents, teachers, and students are interviewed.

Roerden, L. P. (2001). Lessons of the wild. In L. Lantieri (Ed.), *Schools with spirit* (pp. 53–76). Boston: Beacon. This essay documents an outdoor learning program that takes students to scuba dive "the wall" off the Grand Cayman Island.

Root, R. L., Jr., & Steinberg, M. (Eds.). (2005). *The fourth genre: Contemporary writers of/on creative nonfiction* (3rd ed.). New York: Pearson Longman. An edited collection of creative nonfiction essays that can be used as models for readers and writers of nonfiction. The introduction contains a thorough philosophical, theoretical, and practical overview of the genre.

Rose, Mike. (2009). *Why school*. New York: New Press. Rose asks policy makers at all levels of education to reengage with the "ethical, social, and imaginative dimensions of human experience." While he directs us to value "creativity and the majesty of intelligence," he fails to directly name his ideas holistic or spiritual.

Simmons, G. (2003). *The I of the storm: Embracing conflict, creating peace*. Unity Village, MO: Unity House. A process that leads to peacemaking teaches us how to embrace conflict and to use it within the process. The spiritual self, the "I" of the storm, lies at the center of this approach that also integrates a variety of spiritual and scientific concepts.

Tompkins, J. (1996). *A life in school: What the teacher learned*. Reading, MA: Perseus. Tompkins writes a memoir of her years in school. It calls for the need for a holistic approach to education.

Vaughan, F. (1986). *The inward arc: Healing and wholeness in psychotherapy and spirituality*. Boston: Shambhalla. This book is the foundational text for transpersonal psychology. It takes a holistic approach to promoting self-healing. Vaughan posits that spirituality and psychotherapy are complementary.

About the Author and Contributors

Susan A. Schiller, PhD, is director of the MA in humanities program at Central Michigan University as well as professor of English and member of the graduate faculty at Central Michigan University. She teaches composition, American literature, film studies, and English education. She and Gary Babiuk coedit *The Holistic Educator: The Newsletter for the Holistic Learning and Spirituality in Education Professional Interest Community Group of ASCD*. Her research interests include spiritual approaches to writing and learning, holistic education, studies in Willa Cather, and imagery and affect in meaning making. She has published in *Teaching Cather, Mid-America*, the *Journal of the Assembly for Expanded Perspectives on Learning, Innovative Higher Education, Language Arts Journal of Michigan*, and *Transformations*. She and Regina Paxton Foehr are coeditors of *The Spiritual Side of Writing: Releasing the Learner's Whole Potential*, and she and Robert Root cochaired a national conference for the Assembly for Expanded Perspectives on Learning (AEPL) titled "Mapping Nonfiction." She lives in Mount Pleasant, Michigan, with her husband Theopolis L. Gilmore.

Gary Babiuk, PhD, is an assistant professor in the faculty of education at the University of Manitoba in Winnipeg, Canada. He has twenty-three years of experience as a teacher and school administrator and thirteen years as a teacher educator. His current research interests are in inquiry learning and holistic and integrative education as they relate to education for sustainability.

Joy Bracewell, PhD, is working as a Brittain Fellow at the Georgia Institute of Technology in Atlanta. As research coordinator of the Communications Center, she oversees projects on English-language learners (ELL), multimodal communication, and external national grants. Her research interests include transatlantic discourses on the formation of the middle class, reacting to the past pedagogy, and studies in Willa Cather. She also has published articles on how print technology affects conception of race in the nineteenth century.

www.ingramcontent.com/pod-product-compliance
Lightning Source LLC
Chambersburg PA
CBHW051527230426
43668CB00012B/1766